T0167839

OMAHA BEACH 6 JUNE 1944 THE D-DAY LANDING

ROBERT J. PARKER

AMBERLEY

Acknowledgements

I would like to offer thanks to Jonathan Reeve and Jonathan Jackson for their encouragement and enthusiasm in suggesting this project from the earliest stage, and to all of the editorial staff at Amberley Publishing for their energy and effort in completing this volume. That would surely include Connor Stait, Louis Archard, Patricia Curley, and Vicki Fletcher, along with the entire production team. Most importantly, I would dearly love to thank my wife Sheila for her support and patience in the writing of this D-Day series. Any and all errors of fact or interpretation are entirely mine.

RJP
Valparaiso, Indiana

About the Author

Robert J. Parker holds Bachelors and Masters degrees in history. He currently lectures in US history at Purdue University Northwest and has written several books concerning British and American history, including Amberley's *Passchendaele* 1917 and *British Prime Ministers*. He resides in Valparaiso, Indiana, just outside of Chicago, and visits the United Kingdom regularly. He travels extensively and has visited over eighty countries on six continents.

First published 2019

Amberley Publishing
The Hill, Stroud
Gloucestershire, GL5 4EP

www.amberley-books.com

British Library Cataloguing in Publication Data.
A catalogue record for this book is available from the British Library.

ISBN 978 1 4456 6926 7 (paperback)
ISBN 978 1 4456 6927 4 (ebook)

Typesetting and Origination by Amberley Publishing.
Printed in Great Britain.

Contents

Chapter 1

Introduction:
Operation Overlord

The most difficult and complicated operation ever to take place.
British Prime Minister Winston Churchill

6 June 1944 saw the greatest amphibious invasion in history. 7,000 vessels of all sizes, shapes, and functions were gathered near numerous ports and harbours along England's southern coast. Taking to the air over the English Channel were over 7,500 warplanes. Over 200,000 soldiers, sailors and airmen were poised and anxious as they awaited their fate – their mission, to attempt to successfully cross 100 miles of storm-tossed English Channel and establish a gateway into German-occupied France. Amid heaving waves, threatening weather, and in the face of enemy gunfire, the massive Allied armada successfully disembarked 130,000 combat troops, plus an additional 24,000 by air, on a 50-mile-wide set of beaches off the coast of Normandy, France. Remembered today as 'D-Day', this operation was the culmination of two and a half years of planning, preparation and endless debate, controversy and postponement. The success of the Allied re-entry into north-western France would be the springboard for the drive across northern Europe and into the very heartland of Nazi Germany. It would be the initial act of liberation for the captive peoples of France, Belgium, Denmark and the Netherlands, who had been held and terrorised in the grip of Adolf Hitler's Nazi conquest since the spring of 1940.

The decision to launch the invasion in the face of impending bad weather was anything but a given. Even the commitment to embark, engage and conduct the extensive build-up for so huge and overwhelming an enterprise had also been problematic. The demanding necessity to provide a viable 'second front' against Nazi Germany required a vast and unified Allied effort, including: meticulously detailed planning; the physical capacity to provide the essential resources; and the relentless energy to sustain faith in such an enormous endeavour. Frequent postponements due to the lack of material equipment, coupled with the haunting pessimism from the sheer fear of failure given the ominous threat of the Germans pushing the invasion back into the sea, worked to either temporarily impede, or eventually to inspire, its eventual achievement.

Success at Normandy was preceded by the combined factors of: the presence of Allied armies climbing up the spine of Italy to drain German forces from France; the round-the-clock hammering of German cities from sustained Allied air attack; and the violently diabolical war on the Eastern Front, involving over 100 divisions of the Soviet Red Army against an equally large and lethal German Army. With the opening of a legitimate second front, the Germans would be placed in a vice-like grip of strangulation, destruction and defeat.

No part of the Overlord operation would be easy: from planning, to preparation, to implementation. Among the high-stakes decisions to be considered and debated were the selection of the beaches on which to land; the implementation and method for the massive build-up of men, material and equipment; the methodical destruction of German defences before the invasion; and the simultaneous ongoing deceptions as to where and when the actual landings would take place. But in the end, it would be the courageous willingness of each individual soldier and sailor to actually endure the challenge to cross the English Channel and commit to an amphibious landing – an effort that seemed to many a far too insurmountable undertaking, but one that would be memorably and spectacularly fulfilled.

Indeed, some Allied leaders themselves repeatedly questioned the necessity, let alone the chances of success, of such a daunting task – a task deemed by many to be too dangerous and too risky a gamble against the vaunted German Wehrmacht that stood poised to defeat and destroy any attempt at invasion of Hitler's 'Fortress Europe'. D-Day, or more correctly, Operation Overlord, was of course the planned Allied re-entry into Western Europe. With the defeat of France and the expulsion of the British Army from the European continent by the Germans in the spring of 1940, the return to France by Allied forces had come to dominate the strategic thinking of the Allied political leadership and their respective military high commands. While the Soviets engaged the German Army in a deadly struggle of cataclysmic proportions on the vast Eastern Front, the call for a second front to relieve pressure on the hard-pressed Soviets and to re-establish an Allied presence on the western European continent became an issue of growing urgency and debate. With the Japanese bombing of Pearl Harbor in December 1941 and the entry of the United States into the war, the strategic perspective, philosophy and capacity for the proposed Allied invasion became altered, re-energised, and re-oriented.

The debate centred on when, where, and in what form the proposed invasion would take place. The mere attempt to conduct such an enormous amphibious invasion was in itself not automatically assumed in any concrete sense. In fact, the controversy became at times quite hostile to the stability and compatibility of the Allied Powers. This hostility not only included relations between the Soviet Union and her US and British allies, but also between the United States and Great Britain. For the Soviets, the question was one of desperation and resentment. The Red Army was fighting the Nazi war machine on a 2,000-mile front, involving 4 million soldiers, battling in an epic life and death engagement that was devouring a quarter of a million casualties every month. Soviet leader Josef Stalin was pleased to receive mountains of supplies and aid from Britain and the US, but was desperately desiring and eagerly awaiting the opening of the much-promised second front.

For her part, Britain was continuing to endure the hardship of five years of food shortages and lack of basic consumer requirements, while doggedly reminding Stalin that it had been Britain that had stood alone from spring 1940 until Hitler's ill-advised invasion of her virtual ally, Soviet Russia, in June 1941. Britain was now committing everything within her military and economic power to carry on the war effort against Germany. Britain was providing aid to Soviet Russia with equipment and provisions to sustain their war effort, while also conducting determined multiple military actions on several global wartime fronts – although, to Stalin's endless frustration, not the often promised invasion of France.

Britain and the US had invaded North Africa, Sicily and the Italian mainland in an effort not only to engage German troops on the battlefield, but to relieve pressure against the Soviets from the German juggernaut on the Eastern Front. At the same time, Great Britain had dedicated one-third of her domestic economy to an aerial war effort that included the nightly bombing of German targets all over Europe. This prohibitively expensive strategic effort had reduced not only the German capacity to produce war material with which to pursue her war with Soviet Russia, but also drew off enormous amounts of wartime equipment, manpower and production for the air defence of the German homeland. The British and American air forces were conducting virtually round-the-clock bombing of German cities and industry with devastating and doggedly persistent strategic air attacks. Even with these determined endeavours, Stalin considered British and US efforts up to this time as sideshows of little consequence to the overall defeat of Germany. Responding to Soviet Russia, and to the world, President Franklin Roosevelt and the United States remained adamant: there must be, and there would be, a re-entry into north-western France by combined Allied forces – spearheaded by the United States Army. For Roosevelt and his senior advisors, and for the entire war effort, it was a case of the sooner the better.

The US was already committed to providing both Great Britain and Soviet Russia with colossal amounts of food, wartime material and equipment. But at the insistence of British Prime Minister Winston Churchill and the British high command, the US had reluctantly postponed an invasion of France in both 1942 and 1943. This led to the US viewing any further delay with great scepticism. Great Britain's attempt to again postpone the invasion beyond 1944 and into 1945 was seen as a further indication of Britain's reluctance and unwillingness to launch the difficult, but ultimately necessary, enterprise. The US had gradually conceded that France could not be invaded in 1942 or 1943 due to insufficient resources. Therefore, in order to engage the Germans somewhere, they began looking elsewhere. 'We must fight Germans on the battlefield,' proclaimed Roosevelt, and 'anywhere' according to FDR meant agreement to Britain's suggestion to invade North Africa and help the British forces clear the African continent of German threats to the Suez Canal and Mediterranean Sea. Following the successful North African campaign, the Anglo-American forces decided to seize the island of Sicily, and in so doing develop the opportunity to invade the Italian mainland and knock Italy out of the war. This ongoing struggle was achieved through bitter fighting during 1942–43, and Italy had indeed surrendered, although the Germans stubbornly held out in the mountainous boot of the Italian peninsula. Concurrently, the US was pursuing its dedicated engagement to a large and demanding trans-global Pacific war against Japan. For many Americans, both in and out of the military, this sprawling and distant struggle in the Pacific theatre was the correct and overriding confrontation. They considered, due to the Pearl Harbor attack, Japan to be the true aggressor and felt the main objective should be victory in the Pacific. Therefore, for many in the US, the defeat of Imperial Japan deserved the greater bulk of the US war effort and expense.

It was against these hard-nosed obstacles of resources, global strategy and Allied responsibility that the decision to finally invade Western Europe was settled and implemented. Combined Allied discussion and agreement would not be enough. Notwithstanding the conference table debates and head-nodding, and in spite of the ravenous demands for equipment and manpower by every worldwide outpost, the build-up for the Normandy invasion would claim priority. The strategy of 'Germany first' and the commitment to preparation for an invasion of unprecedented size, scope and dimension would be the primary focus of Britain and America. As daunting and difficult as these strategic and material challenges were, the US nonetheless anxiously sought the moment for the most immediate and aggressive method to attack and defeat Germany: the invasion of north-west France. By the spring of 1944, that moment had arrived.

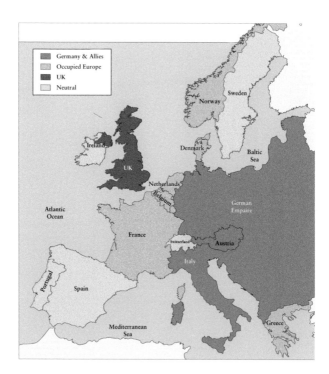

Western Europe during much of the Second World War suffered under Nazi occupation. Britain's island location was essential in preventing German victory.

Above: 'The Big Three' (Stalin, Roosevelt and Churchill) meeting at the Tehran Conference in December 1943. It was here that Roosevelt announced the spring 1944 date for the D-Day landing and the supreme commander for Operation Overlord. This information encouraged Stalin concerning the Allied commitment, but it would be another six months, and more delays, before execution. (LOC)

Left: Adolf Hitler single-handedly controlled virtually every aspect of German diplomatic and military strategy. It was Hitler and the Nazi domination of Europe that the Allies were desperate to eliminate. By 1944, with the lurking danger of a successful Allied invasion, Hitler was seriously confronted by the possibility of a major second Allied front. (NARA)

The present-day American military cemetery above Omaha Beach at Colleville-sur-Mer. The Allies suffered a combined 10,000 casualties during the D-Day assault, with roughly 4,400 killed. (RJP)

A typical 'big gun' battery located along the French coast. The problem for the Germans was that they did not know what part of the French coast would be invaded, and which would need such weapons; therefore, the entire French coast received fortification. (Bundesarchiv)

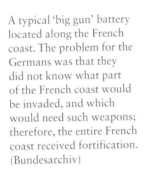

A heavily fortified German observation bunker atop Pont du Hoc, overlooking the American 'Omaha' invasion beach. (RJP)

German Panzer divisions would pose an enormous threat to the Allied invasion if they could be rapidly brought to bear from their reserve position to the rear and engage upon identification of an invasion force. This tactic proved to be faulty during the actual invasion due to hesitation on the part of the German high command. (Bundesarchiv)

The scattered veteran German units manning Hitler's 'Atlantic Wall' would prove to be stubborn foes throughout the Normandy campaign, but especially on D-Day at Omaha Beach. (NARA)

Stalin and German Foreign Minister Joachim Ribbentrop agreeing to the infamous Nazi-Soviet Pact in 1939, prior to the start of the Second World War. Hitler then invaded Soviet Russia in June 1941, placing Stalin in the Allied camp and creating a devastating war on the Eastern Front. Hitler now sought to avoid a second front in the west, while Stalin demanded one from Great Britain and America. (LOC)

Above left: Franklin Roosevelt had been pressing for an Allied invasion of north-west Europe since the American entry into the Second World War in December 1941. (LOC)

Above right: Josef Stalin had also been desperately urging an Allied second front since the German invasion of the Soviet Union in June 1941. He was increasingly suspicious of Allied reluctance to embark on this enterprise. (LOC)

Right: Prime Minister Winston Churchill had heroically kept Britain fighting during the early part of the Second World War. He remained gravely concerned about the difficulty and feasibility of an Allied invasion of France. (LOC)

Chapter 2

Why Omaha Beach?

Allied planners hated the idea of assaulting Omaha Beach, but it had to be done. This was as obvious to Rommel as to Eisenhower.

Military historian Stephen Ambrose

The D-Day invasion strategy involving five French beaches in Normandy offered many advantages that other candidates for invasion significantly lacked. The Pas de Calais area was of course closer to England, but was also more heavily defended and offered absolutely no element of surprise. Calais was confined to a narrow area for Allied reinforcement to any depth, and all transport coming or going, especially the initial assault, would be easily exposed to German observation and attack, and therefore exceedingly dangerous and difficult. As long as the designated target area of Normandy maintained its element of surprise, it would provide Overlord with a considerable set of advantages for invasion compared to the Pas de Calais.

Another alternative landing site, offering potential for both surprise and a major deep-water harbour, was the Cotentin Peninsula with its desirable port of Cherbourg. However, again there were problems. Assuming the element of surprise was maintained, the fighting would be contained to a narrow peninsula which would be much easier for the Germans to block before the Allies could spread out east into the open French countryside. There was also no guarantee that an attack on the Cotentin Peninsula would necessarily roll up and capture Cherbourg intact. An intact port under siege would be very easy for the Germans to destroy with demolitions before surrendering, even assuming the successful invasion of the Cotentin area. In the event, Cherbourg was indeed captured, but was virtually demolished before the Allies could occupy it.

Therefore Normandy, with its broad and hopefully lightly defended beaches, offered the best combination of surprise and quick access to open country. The 50-mile invasion zone also offered space to reinforce a planned 500,000-man army and its voracious appetite for equipment and supplies.

To break out of this 50-mile swath of Normandy coast would require depth of penetration and the immediate arrival of more troops, armour and supplies. The one beach location that offered the greatest potential for penetration into the interior, along with the widest variety of access roads, was the beach designated Omaha. Once onto the shingle of beach and bluffs overlooking the sea, the area provided ample opportunity to connect with nearby roads and junctions, cutting into the interior of the Normandy area. This would be vital if the initial landing was going to properly develop into a full-scale invasion of France, followed by the bigger push across the Rhine and into Germany.

Adequate ports and re-supply capability would be essential, but the original pivot point of introduction would be important for the wings to swing off of the flanks, cut off the Cotentin Peninsula, and access a fully functioning harbour at Cherbourg. Assuming the flanks along the 50-mile invasion beach could be secured, it would then be up to the American troops landing on Omaha Beach to access its nearby diverse road system to accommodate and forward the increased reinforcement of troops and supplies. Unfortunately, Omaha was probably the most ruggedly fortified and held of all five beaches. Worse for the invasion forces, Omaha provided the Germans with a dominant defensive advantage in terms of cliffs, bluffs and heights, and field of fire.

The Germans had reasoned that if Normandy was chosen for invasion, then the Omaha Beach area would need to be the 'gateway' for transport opportunity. This recognition led to a thoroughly well-designed system of concrete encasements, machine-gun nests, bunkers and crossfire development. An even bigger risk would be the approach. Both flanks of Omaha Beach were lined with cliffs and to the south-west of Omaha Beach proper were the high cliffs of Pont du Hoc with their heavily fortified bunkers teeming with big gun emplacements. Should approach vessels advance toward the Omaha sector, the landing ships would be under intense fire from the offshore batteries at Pont du Hoc. In other words, Omaha offered the greatest opportunity for the Normandy invasion follow-up, and its location was indeed essential, but Omaha also presented the greatest danger and difficulty in acquisition and would be the most costly and difficult of the five beach assaults. The hopes and the fears of the Omaha sector would all be murderously realised.

Omaha Beach is shaped in a 'new moon' crescent, with 100-foot-high cliffs on both ends, and the Germans had studded it with concrete bunkers and big guns. The Allied plan was to attack the cliffs separately, knock out the guns and protect the flanks to the invasion beach. The beach itself was broad and low, heavily mined and forested with hundreds of 'dragons' teeth' steel obstacles, many capped with mines. The beach itself washed over 1,000 yards at low tide to a low shingle, and then more beach to a 100-foot bluff and ridge, covered with sagebrush and bristling with German machine-gun nests. At each corner of the beach, and along the centre bluffs, sat several concrete bunkers and pillboxes armed with powerful mid-range artillery, such as the notorious 88 millimetre flak gun, and a variety of mixed machine guns. These outposts were manned by crews of defenders of up to 1,000 to 1,500 troops. The key would be to reduce these bristling defences by ship and aircraft bombardment, storm the beaches with an overwhelming assault force, secure the beach before the Germans could reinforce with nearby Panzer divisions of mobile armoured units and tanks, and then rapidly pour in more men and heavy equipment. Such was the plan.

Omaha Beach proved to be the most heavily defended of the five beaches, both in numbers of defenders and in strength of guns, amplified by the natural defensive terrain of bluffs and ridges. The flat beach, protected by a long run to the high bluffs, was a natural defensive position for the German defenders. The array of German defensive equipment at Omaha, in terms of anti-tank guns alone, was over three times the number on the four other Normandy beaches. Omaha would greet the assault teams with eighty-five machine-gun nests as compared to an average of twenty to thirty on the other four beaches, and two artillery battalions compared to one or less at the other four sites.

In short, of the five beaches, Omaha offered the toughest attack location, the stiffest beach defences of German guns of all types and the heaviest numbers of German defenders. It was a lethal combination to go up against – especially considering the fact that the assault was coming from the sea and arriving in dangerously vulnerable landing craft. Further compounding the already difficult situation, the pre-landing naval bombardment scheduled for Omaha was shorter and later than at the other beaches due to the tidal restrictions that this location entailed. Nature presented other obstacles that negatively impacted the actual invasion: the air bombardment was lighter than anticipated due to low cloud cover that would prevent adequate air assault, and Allied landing forces would be unable to get the American armour ashore in good order due to rough seas. All of these factors gave Omaha Beach its grim challenge and, later, its deadly reputation.

In the early planning stages of the Overlord operation, Omaha Beach had been selected not only for its advantageous location but also because intelligence information indicated it was lightly defended. Early reconnaissance had shown few defenders manning the fortifications at Omaha. Throughout the spring of 1944, however, conditions had been radically altered by Field Marshal Erwin Rommel. Rommel and the German high command had recently sought to increase and strengthen the overall defensive perimeter of Hitler's European 'Atlantic Wall' and in particular those areas beyond the Pas de Calais strong points. Earlier, US planners had determined that, due to its terrain and adjoining bluffs, if Omaha Beach was defended by at least one full infantry division of German defenders, it would be virtually impregnable to an offshore beach assault. Such were the mixed pre-invasion conclusions, both for and against selecting the Omaha site.

Unfortunately, right up to the June invasion date, the Allied intelligence teams remained convinced that Omaha was only thinly defended with but one lightly armed defending regiment backed up by modest reinforcement capability. In reality, the Germans had placed more than three times that strength in the Omaha area.

Omaha Beach was essential to the Overlord scheme, but it would be a deadly challenge requiring courageous sacrifice, heroism and the utmost determination on the part of the American soldier and sailor in order to succeed.

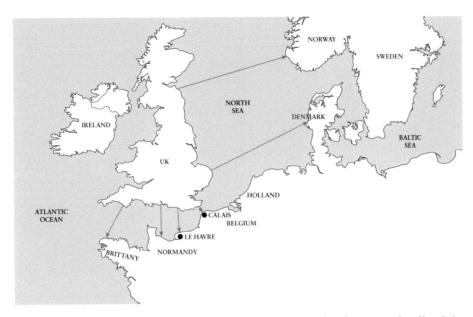

Many potential invasion routes to liberate Europe were considered. Normandy offered the greatest combination of assets and chances for success.

US soldiers rehearsing beach landings in Britain prior to D-Day. (LOC)

American soldiers getting ready to board D-Day transports in Weymouth. Several GIs are seen with Bangalore torpedoes over their shoulders. (NARA)

American sailors and soldiers loading equipment onto various transport vessels prior to D-Day. American shipyards had been rapidly constructing hundreds of transport vessels to provide adequate 'lift' for the Normandy invasion. The global war required an enormous industrial capacity to manufacture and transport tons of equipment, supplies and weapons around the world. (NARA)

Literally hundreds of fully loaded transports waiting to cross the English Channel prior to D-Day. (NARA)

American Sherman 'wading' tanks being loaded onto landing craft prior to D-Day. These tanks featured air intakes, allowing the vehicles to enter and wade through the low surf and negotiate the invasion beach. (NARA)

The crescent-shaped Omaha Beach that invading American soldiers would be required to cross on D-Day. Unlike today, the beach would be lined with obstacles and mines, and blanketed with gunfire from the surrounding bluffs. (RJP)

German big gun bunkers overlooking the English Channel and located just east of Omaha Beach at Longues-sur-Mer. (RJP)

Chapter 3

Overlord Commanders

The Supreme Commander has to sit on a very lofty perch and be able to take a detached view of the whole intricate problem.

> British General Sir Bernard Montgomery on the importance and responsibilities of the Eisenhower's position as Overlord commander

Political leaders make grand policy and appoint the commanders. Commanders attempt to achieve in the field the desired results envisioned by their superiors, the decision-makers. Those commanders entrusted to carry out these great plans rely on skill, organisation, experience and, inevitably, good fortune. For the Normandy invasion, the chain of command descended cleanly and directly from President Franklin Roosevelt to General George Marshall and to the person placed in supreme command of the overall operation, General Dwight D. Eisenhower. The thread could not have been sharper and more direct.

Roosevelt was following his own intuition to seize the offensive and attack and conquer Nazi Germany. Plus, he had made a promise to Soviet Russia's leader, Josef Stalin, that a second front on the continent of Europe would be opened as soon as possible. Stalin was notorious for frequently and persistently accusing the Western Allies of reneging on their commitment to the second front, if not in word of promise then in speed of delivery. Certainly, British Prime Minister Winston Churchill and his commanders were in no hurry to attack the Germans with an invasion of France. British strategists had pursued what Stalin and Roosevelt deemed 'sideshows' in North Africa, Sicily and Italy. Churchill and his generals feared and respected not only the fighting capability of the German Wehrmacht, but also the risk of being thrown back into the sea from the beaches, or engaging in a battle with horrific First World War casualties for no territorial gain. The American contingent, however, led by Roosevelt's most trusted military advisor, George Marshall, was confident and adamant in support of Roosevelt's belief that only by engaging the Germans in Northern France and driving into the German heartland would Nazi Germany be defeated. Marshall not only believed in the policy but was confident that it would succeed under the weight of combined Allied strength and force of commitment. Therefore, the emphasis on invading France was gradually gaining traction due to the enormous American build-up of men and arms. Dwarfing the British contribution, this American dominance in men, material and resources would leverage the British into a back seat, strategically and tactically, and thrust the American energy for invasion into high gear. This became the overall Allied policy – whether Churchill and the British approved it or not. For Roosevelt and Marshall, the invasion of France and assault on Hitler's vaunted 'Fortress Europe' was to be the only policy that mattered. The appointment of Eisenhower as the commander of the cross-Channel assault underscored the depth of American commitment and investment, and the sooner it began, the quicker the war would be brought to an end.

Eisenhower had not been predicted as an early choice for supreme commander. Churchill favoured his own top military advisor, the Chief of the Imperial General Staff (CIGS) General Sir Alan Brooke. Roosevelt assuredly felt that George Marshall deserved and could handle such a responsibility. Neither Brooke nor Marshall, however, would be chosen. For Brooke it was an openly crushing decision and bitterly disappointing. But as Churchill pointed out, and Brooke reluctantly agreed, it was to be an 'American show'. For Marshall, the reasoning had to do with FDR's reliance on someone in Washington DC who could manage the entire war effort. In FDR's own words, 'I could not sleep at ease if [he] were out of Washington.' Ever the loyal soldier and advisor, Marshall concurred.[1]

So in December of 1943, and in agreement with the other Allies, a spring 1944 invasion date was finally set. FDR then announced that, with Marshall's firm recommendation, it would be Eisenhower in the supreme command position. This announcement partially pacified the anxious Stalin, who had again questioned the resolve of Britain and the US for want of a definite date and a commanding officer for the invasion. This then settled the question as to when it would occur and who would be in charge.

Before the Second World War, Eisenhower had never led troops in active combat but had gradually risen through the ranks in a variety of pre-war administrative posts. His rise during the Second World War accelerated as Marshall recognised Eisenhower's talents and potential, appointing him as Chief of Operations, then Commander of European Theatre Operations, and eventually commander of Operation Torch during the invasion of North Africa. This was followed quickly by the elevation to supreme commander for the invasion of Sicily and then Italy, and finally chief of Western Allied Operations in Europe. Eisenhower's meteoric rise and string of Mediterranean successes then led to his appointment by Marshall and approval by FDR as the Supreme Commander for the Overlord invasion.

Though lacking in battlefield campaign experience, Eisenhower was brilliant at organisation and administration. Combined with his naturally genial personality, he became particularly adept at getting Allied co-commanders to work together. This was critically important when dealing with the British and French commanders who would be serving with him. Diplomacy, compromise and leadership would be his strongest attributes – and as many later observers would agree, the most critically important feature to his success. To carry out such a huge operation as Overlord would take superior diplomatic, organisational and administrative skills that involved meshing a wide range of divergent personalities, egos and talents. In this, Eisenhower was unfailing.

Eisenhower is sometimes criticised for lacking bold tactical awareness and imagination, but his selection of operational commanders easily outweighs that rebuke. Eisenhower was ruthless in the dismissal of officers who could not, or would not, perform to his full expectations. Correctly choosing capable subordinates who functioned as a war-winning team was of paramount importance. To this strength Eisenhower added patience, skill, and at times even genius. It was said that Eisenhower made it all look easy, but of course it wasn't easy; it was demanding, difficult and arduous. To criticise by saying it appeared to be easy only further emphasises the inherent qualities that Eisenhower possessed.

Eisenhower astutely blended his staff with both British and American officers – and this went beyond mere window dressing. Eisenhower sought and followed the advice of his commanders, even those who were less than congenial in their personalities, such as the vain and arrogant British General Sir Bernard Montgomery. At times insufferable, even for his fellow British commanders, Montgomery was appreciated by Eisenhower for his methodical planning and battlefield preparation. Eisenhower named Montgomery as the overall ground commander for the invasion and readily agreed with Montgomery that the original invasion plan was too narrow and would need to be widened to include two more beaches and two more divisions. Such was the trust that Eisenhower placed in his staff.

Reflecting the confidence shown by Roosevelt's appointment and Marshall's enthusiastic recommendation, Eisenhower now began selecting those to assist him in the logistical and tactical details for the upcoming invasion. It would be necessary to meld both American and British officers into these vital positions; it would also be important to find room for the leaders of the Free French Army, since it was France that was going to be invaded and trampled upon by the Allied forces. Liberation was important, but so too was French participation in the actual event, and this would require involving their self-proclaimed head, the onerously vainglorious General Charles de Gaulle. Although certainly brave and courageously loyal to France, de Gaulle was roundly despised by both Roosevelt and Churchill for his pomposity and interference in Allied affairs.[2]

Eisenhower's positive relationship with Britain's Prime Minister Winston Churchill would be essential. Although they frequently disagreed on both policy and method, they retained a mutual trust and respect that included an amiable fondness for each other. Eisenhower quickly and liberally assembled a mix of British and American officers in his upper echelon invasion team – pleasing and satisfying both Roosevelt and Churchill. In his instructions to Eisenhower, Marshall was explicit: Eisenhower would get any officers he required, and his appointments would be fully granted. However, Ike was not to hesitate in the removal of any officer he felt inadequate to the task at hand or who failed to meet his satisfaction. Eisenhower would receive full support in his requests for subordinates, manpower and resources.

For his Deputy Supreme Commander, Eisenhower chose British Air Chief Marshal Sir Arthur Tedder. Air power would be vital in all stages of the invasion, and it was essential to have a dedicated airman responsible for invasion priorities and requests on tactics and allotted resources. Disputes over the use and command of air power for the invasion would be bitter and constant, but in the end, Eisenhower and the invasion requirements would get the nod.

Eisenhower chose his own personal friend and confidant as Chief of Staff, Major General Walter Bedell ('Beetle') Smith. Smith was thorough, professional and efficient, respected by all for his excellence. The Assistant Chief of Staff would be the British General Sir Frederick Morgan, who had formerly headed up the invasion planning committee before the appointment of Eisenhower.

For his Army Group Commander on the ground, Eisenhower chose the talented but highly egotistical British General Sir Bernard Montgomery. Ike and Monty had clashed before, but it could not be denied that the latter was a dedicated and meticulous planner. Even though Churchill was at times exasperated by Montgomery, Monty had won the Battle of El Alamein against Rommel and the Germans in North Africa, and Churchill and the British were desperate for victories over the Germans. To Montgomery would go the task of planning the details of the beach landings and troop depositions – the bread and butter of the entire invasion plan.

Eisenhower chose British Air Chief Marshal Sir Trafford Leigh-Mallory to be in charge of the Allied invasion air forces and British Admiral Sir Bertram Ramsey to be in charge of the vital naval arm of the invasion forces. It had been Ramsey who coordinated the rescue of the British Army from Dunkirk in the spring of 1940, and he would now organise the massive flotilla of Allied ships to deliver the Allies back into France – Operation Neptune.

Eisenhower's adroit appointment of British officers for the top three command posts (ground, air and naval) did much to reassure Churchill and other British senior officers that Eisenhower was going to be fair and pragmatic in his selection for the combined operation. The individual army groups would retain their own national identities and officers, but the vast overall operation would be combined under one single upper command, the Chief of Staff, Supreme Allied Headquarters (COSSAC), now to be renamed Supreme Headquarters, Allied Expeditionary Force (SHAEF), of which Eisenhower assumed command.

OMAHA BEACH COMMAND

The British command of the 'eastern beaches', labelled Gold, Sword, and Juno, would have a separate set of naval, infantry and airborne commanders while remaining under the unified command of Eisenhower and his SHAEF staff. Likewise, the American sector or 'western beaches', consisting of Omaha Beach, Utah Beach and Pont du Hoc, was also under the overall SHAEF command, although the immediate direct command was given to Lieutenant General Omar Bradley. Bradley had been Eisenhower's trusted battlefield commander from the Mediterranean campaigns and his 'western beaches' group, designated First US Army, would then be divided again under two component sets of commanders: Major General J. Lawton Collins would head the Utah Beach infantry and airborne landings, conducted by his VII Corps, and Major General Leonard T. Gerow's V Corps would land at nearby Omaha Beach and secure Pont du Hoc. The US naval commander assigned to bombard the 'western' beaches and land the American forces was Admiral Alan Kirk. Kirk's 'western' task force would again be divided into two forces: the Omaha sector headed by Admiral John Hall and the Utah sector headed by Admiral Don Moon.

GERMAN COMMAND

German control can be succinctly summed up in their leader, Adolf Hitler. Hitler not only made policy, he hired, fired and re-hired his commanders in a continuous circus of appointments. It was, of course, Hitler who had plunged Europe into war in 1939, and now jeopardised his successful conquest of western and central Europe with his ill-advised invasion of Soviet Russia in June 1941. Hitler continued to plague his generals with his maniacal decisions that went against the advice of almost all of his subordinate commanders and advisors. It was already clear that the war in the east against the Soviets was doomed, and that if an Allied invasion of France was successful, there would be no hope for victory or a negotiated peace.

To this end, Hitler required and demanded nothing less than a victory against an Allied invasion of Western Europe. Most of his advisors believed strongly that the Allied attack would indeed come at the Pas de Calais, although Hitler himself was unsure and therefore insisted that his reserve Panzer units wait for his word before engaging. This went completely contrary to the arguments of Hitler's chosen commander for the defence of France against an Allied invasion, Field Marshal Erwin Rommel. Rommel, the famed 'Desert Fox', was an exponent of the mobile Blitzkrieg tactics that he had used so successfully earlier in the war against France and again in North Africa against the British. However, Rommel was now assigned a purely defensive situation with limited options for manoeuvre. Rommel believed that the invasion would have to be defeated on the beaches or the battle would be as good as lost. If the Allies achieved a foothold, then there would be no denying them inevitable victory. To this end, Rommel's plan to defend France, or Hitler's so-called 'Fortress Europe', was to make the coastal beaches as difficult as possible for a landing, and then to immediately engage the invaders and drive the Allies back into the sea. These shore defences would consist of mines, beach obstacles, concrete bunkers, barbed wire and embedded gun emplacements. Twenty divisions of various strength and experience were thinly scattered along the length of the Atlantic coast, reinforced by over two dozen mobile Panzer units. This mammoth 200-mile project was in the midst of being constructed as the Allied invasion arrived in June 1944.

Rommel and the Germans had already laid over 6.5 million mines and thousands of tons of steel-reinforced concrete bunkers, but the French coast was too long, and the time required too limited, and, most important of all, the available manpower and resources to construct enough bunkers and obstacles were entirely lacking. There was also the desperate need for experienced soldiers to man the beach outposts. Castoffs, foreign enlistees, forced labourers, recovering wounded, and re-fitting regiments littered the defensive positions. Worse still for Rommel and the Germans was the limited amount of first-rate soldiers available for combat – the numbers were just no longer there.[3]

Rommel also had respect for his oncoming invading adversaries:

> Our friends from the East [generals in Berlin and those fighting the Soviet armies on the eastern front who to Rommel were out of touch with reality] cannot imagine what they're in for here. It's not a matter of fanatical hordes to be driven forward in masses against our line, with no regard for casualties and little recourse to tactical craft; here we are facing an enemy who applies all his native intelligence to the use of his main technical resources, who spares no expenditure of material and whose every operation goes its course as though it had been the subject of repeated rehearsal![4]

Rommel, like many other German generals, frequently quarrelled with Hitler, although Rommel also clashed with his immediate supervisor, Field Marshal Gerd von Rundstedt, on the positioning of the reinforcing units and the decision of how soon to engage a beach invasion. They all realised that moving forces to defend a deception would be tantamount to a defeat. This question was never conclusively resolved by the German high command. Of the two schools of thought, Rommel's was probably correct, although it required a 'Fortress' approach to every beach and stretch of French coast – an almost impossible task. Certainly the flexible plan of von Rundstedt and Heinz Guderian, another leading German general and frequent critic of Hitler, to hold back the major force of defending Panzer units until it became clear just where the actual invasion strength was centred would require fewer beach defences – but this plan would also require greater numbers of soldiers and tanks in order to attain superior concentration of force when implemented. This, of course, also required the element of time in order to identify where and to what degree the Allies were attacking, and then to rapidly attack those points of invasion when identified. Most importantly, it required sufficient strength to defeat a rapidly reinforcing army of invaders. Another major flaw in this view was the Allies' complete control of the air with its tactical and strategic advantage. In bombers, fighters and fighter-bombers, the Allies owned the air, and nothing could move on the ground without risk of both observation and immediate obliteration. Even assuming the idea to hold back the reserve Panzer units was correct, there was not a thing they could do to guarantee a safe advance of the units to a point of attack. Any movement would expose their location, resulting in a hurricane of withering attack and annihilation. The German air force, the Luftwaffe, was virtually non-existent and had nothing to offer in the form of resistance to the overwhelming Allied air superiority in all types and numbers of planes.

Presented with these circumstances, Rommel's tactics were probably the most practical and correct.

Rommel was obsessed with defending the entire length of the French coast from north of Calais to the southern shore of the Bay of Biscay, even though he realised his forces and resources were inadequate. For Rommel, it was either defeat the Allies on the beach or be defeated. The tactical debate with Hitler and his fellow officers, however, was never settled. The hesitation and confusion on the part of the Germans became greater than the Allies' confusion upon landing, and certainly worked to the Allies' benefit. By failing to fully commit to either strategy, the Germans virtually ensured failure in the primary goal: to defend Europe from a successful invasion. For the Allies, as slender and as risky as they viewed their overall chances of success, neither their determination in preparation before the invasion, nor their dedication when entering the fight on the beaches, ever flagged.

With these opposing forces in place, Operation Neptune was about to commence. This crossing of the English Channel and landing of the Allied forces would inaugurate the D-Day invasion. The long-planned Operation Overlord was ready to begin.

Britain's military high command: Generals Alan Brooke (left) and Bernard Montgomery (right) and British Prime Minister Winston Churchill (centre). Churchill and Brooke remained dubious and hesitant about the Overlord mission and its risks. (NARA)

General Frederick Morgan. Morgan had been in charge of the original planning of the strategy, tactics, and location for Overlord (COSSAC). When Eisenhower became supreme commander for Overlord (SHAEF), he included Morgan as his deputy chief of staff. (NARA)

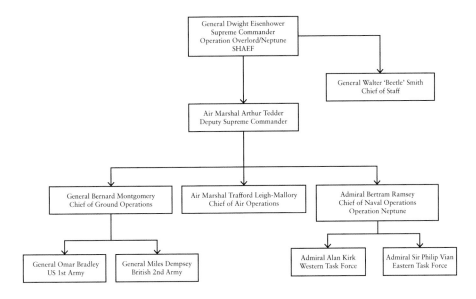

Supreme Headquarters Allied Expeditionary Force (SHAEF) command structure.

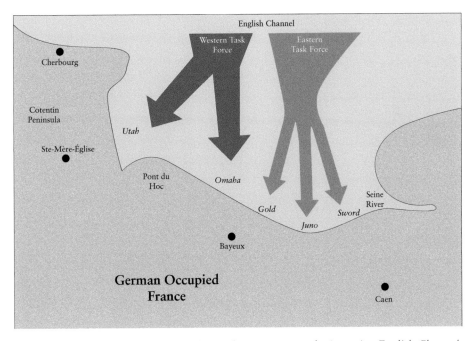

Operation Neptune ferried the Allied assault teams across the imposing English Channel, supported the five beaches with heavy bombardment and delivered the invasion forces into France.

General George Marshall. Marshall remained FDR's most important military advisor through the course of the Second World War. It was Marshall who continually pressured Britain for an Allied invasion of France, and later provided the strong recommendation for Dwight Eisenhower as supreme commander. Marshall had aspired to being the supreme commander for Overlord, but ceded to FDR's wish for Marshall to remain in Washington, D.C. (US Army)

Eisenhower and his chief deputies for Operation Overlord. From left to right, back row: Omar Bradley, Bertram Ramsey, Trafford Leigh-Mallory, Walter 'Beetle' Smith. From left to right, front row: Arthur Tedder, Dwight Eisenhower and Bernard Montgomery. Eisenhower had chosen numerous British officers as essential members of his command team. Tedder (a British air chief marshal) was to be his deputy commander for Operation Overlord. Eisenhower understood the importance of air superiority for the D-Day effort, and Tedder became essential to Ike's command team. (US Navy)

General Bernard Montgomery. Montgomery had defeated Rommel in North Africa, winning the important battle of El Alamein. He was Eisenhower's first choice to be overall ground commander for Operation Overlord. It was Montgomery and Eisenhower who expanded Morgan's three-beach plan into the five-beach invasion strategy that became Operation Overlord. (NARA)

Operation Overlord's infantry high command. In the centre is the chief ground forces commander, Bernard Montgomery; he is flanked by Omar Bradley (left), commander of US ground forces, and Thomas Dempsey, commander of British ground forces. Bradley had been General Eisenhower's lead commander in the North Africa campaign and would remain in command of US ground forces for Operation Overlord. Throughout D-Day morning, the critically desperate situation on Omaha Beach led Bradley to consider withdrawing the invasion forces from Omaha. (US Army)

German General Erwin Rommel, 'The Desert Fox'. In North Africa he had demonstrated his talent for mobile armoured warfare. Now Rommel had been personally selected by Hitler to strengthen Fortress Europa, Hitler's vaunted Atlantic Wall defending against the Allied invasion of Western Europe. In the six months leading up to D-Day he notably increased the defensive strength, with the liberal use of mines and obstacles. (LOC)

Above left: Admiral Alan Kirk, in charge of the US naval operations for the western sector of Operation Overlord. The naval component was Operation Neptune: the crossing of the English Channel for the landing of the US forces on Omaha and Utah Beaches. (US Navy)

Above right: General Leonard Gerow, commander of American ground forces on Omaha Beach for D-Day. (US Army)

Left: General Walter 'Beetle' Smith, Eisenhower's chief of staff for Operation Overlord. Smith was highly regarded and respected by both the American and British high commands. (US Army)

Admiral Sir Bertram Ramsey, Eisenhower's supreme naval commander for Operation Neptune, the vital crossing of the English Channel and landings for Operation Overlord. Ramsey had already won great fame and plaudits for his achievement in rescuing the defeated British Army from Dunkirk in 1940. (NARA)

General Alan Brooke conferring with Eisenhower and Churchill. Brooke and Churchill were reluctant to concede that the war was becoming a larger and increasingly American operation due to the mountains of equipment and supplies being provided, and the rapidly growing size and commitment of the US Army. Brooke thought himself a complete realist towards strategy in general and Overlord in particular. He was forever reining in Churchill from his wilder schemes. Brooke, like Marshall, desired to be the supreme commander of Operation Overlord and was bitterly disappointed to be denied this position. He remained Churchill's chief military advisor through most of the Second World War. (US Army)

General Dwight D. Eisenhower. Eisenhower had never commanded large forces until his rapid rise during the Second World War. For Eisenhower it was imperative that his commanders exude only confidence and optimism in the Overlord project. His administrative and diplomatic talents were outstanding, especially in the role of supreme commander for Operation Overlord. He would later be twice elected as US President on the strength of his wartime successes. (US Army)

Chapter 4

Deception

Very little reliable news came out of England … nothing we learnt gave us a definite clue where the invasion was actually coming.

German General Gunther Blumentritt,
Field Marshal Gerd von Rundstedt's Chief of Staff

Critical to the Allied success was the need for absolute secrecy as to where in France the landings would take place. The most obvious location for this invasion was the Pas de Calais in France, a mere 21 miles from England across the Strait of Dover at the far eastern end of the English Channel. Everything about Calais made it a prime target for an Allied invasion: proximity for ships, planes and the invading soldiers, plus the post-invasion requirements for re-supply and the provision for reinforcement of land units. It was the location that most German commanders believed would be the site of the Allied invasion. Therefore, the nearby Pas de Calais, with its numerous deep-water harbours, became the strongest and most heavily defended area on Hitler's 'Fortress Europe' Atlantic Wall.

Since the Allies would not be invading at Calais, it was essential that the entire mask of delusion accomplish two things: convince the Germans that the Allies would attack at Calais, and secondly, keep the true site of their invasion absolutely secret. For this ruse to be effective, the use of subterfuge in every conceivable aspect, along with rigorously enforced secrecy, had to be diligently maintained. The group of deceptions, compositely known as Operation Bodyguard, would be an integral part of the Overlord operation, and both would be splendidly accomplished.

There were several methods to achieve these two goals, and many coincided with each other. The air strikes by Allied warplanes over France were increased in number and intensity as the D-Day invasion approached, but at the same time they were intentionally concentrated more and more on the Calais area. This further promoted the Nazi belief in a Calais area landing zone. To enhance German confusion and doubt, the raids on other potential target areas were also increased: Le Havre and Normandy in France, but also the farther away possibilities such as Norway and Denmark. All of these potential targets were struck at a lesser ratio than the Calais attacks, which always received at least two thirds of the bomb-drop tonnage.

The secondary efforts at deception involved fake spies, false radio messages and former German spies (now captured and secretly 'turned' to work for the Allies) supplying incorrect data back to the Third Reich. Early in the war, German spies in England had been quietly identified and rounded up. Without Germany's knowledge, they were now entirely under the control of the Allies. Other methods of disinformation ranged from the bizarre to the perverse. Bodies of dead soldiers, with fake papers and fake D-Day information, were cleverly placed or dumped for the Germans to stumble upon and draw false conclusions.

Not to be discounted was the invaluable information obtained by Britain's Bletchley Park codebreakers, who tediously deciphered the German 'Enigma' messages. The Enigma cipher machine was Germany's top secret device for sending coded messages. It was thought by the Germans to be so technically advanced that it would be absolutely impossible for its encryption system to be penetrated and its messages deciphered. Germany went the entire Second World War falsely believing that its coded messages were inviolate. Although not available at all times due to the complexity of the system, the breaking of the Enigma code was an enormous advantage to the Allies throughout the war – and the ability to intercept Enigma messages was one of the greatest secrets held by the Allies, who used the information sparingly in order to preserve its integrity. Only the very highest members of the UK and US governments were privy to its content, referred to as 'Ultra' by the British and 'Magic' by the US, and fewer still to the identity of its source. The breaking of the Enigma code was of particular importance in the Battle of the Atlantic and the elimination the German U-boat threat – another interlocking and vital factor in the success of Operation Overlord.

Finally, the umbrella over all of this deception was the strictly enforced shroud of secrecy maintained by the Allies and their chain of command concerning any and all details of the Overlord plan. Few knew the details of the overall plan, and individual units did not learn of their actual specific targets until D-Day. Planning and training missions were conducted with mock and fictitious names, while masking the true identities of beach and assault locations.

One prominent exception to the tight security blanket was actually part of the deception: the attention given to the arrival, basing and training of General George Patton's 'First US Invasion Group' (FUSAG). Code named Operation Fortitude, this fake unit, and its mass of phoney equipment, was intentionally left quasi-open to view. The clever placement of Patton, the commander that the Germans believed should and would lead the invasion, led the Germans to wrongly conclude that Patton was preparing the invasion force and was primed to attack directly across the Strait of Dover at the Pas de Calais. The Germans were not surprised to learn that Patton had arrived in England to prepare and train an army, and Patton's presence gave credence to the bogus 'First US Invasion Group' army. Patton's phantom army drew German reconnaissance attention, encouraging false conclusions through the observation of mock equipment consisting of cardboard and balloon props near the coast of Dover across the Channel from German-held Calais. Arriving in England, Patton made public appearances, and was training his Third Army for eventual combat in Europe, but of course these units were not the actual invasion force. The fake 'First

US Invasion Group' was impressively backed up by dummy camps, barracks, planes, tanks and armoured vehicles that were only partially camouflaged. All of this was to further impress on the Germans, and any would-be spies or reconnaissance elements, that Patton and his army were preparing to attack at Calais.

Rommel and the main German commanders, such as the overall commander Field Marshal Gerd von Rundstedt of the Central Defense Region, all concluded that Calais was to be the target, although Hitler himself always had a suspicion that the Allies might attempt another location. This belief and conviction that the invasion would be somewhere around Calais was so tightly held that it was two days after D-Day before the Germans fully realised that Normandy was not a feint, and that they must concentrate their reserve Panzer divisions against the Normandy area. By then the initiative for a rapid counterattack that could destroy the invasion was lost. German troops had remained in passive reserve too long, while their commanders stubbornly clung to their faith in a Calais target.

The Allies succeeded in both maintaining the secrecy of the Normandy location and generating confusion as to whether it was the true invasion. Such hesitation cost the Germans their opportunity to drive the Allied invasion force back into the sea, as Rommel had insisted would be necessary if the invasion was to be defeated. The plan for deception and secrecy had worked; now it was up to the real invasion forces to successfully carry out the true invasion in Normandy.

At the Bletchley Park decoding centre, prototype computer-like machines known as 'bombes' would churn through the coded Enigma intercepts to ferret out deciphered German messages. (RJP)

Bletchley Park, the decoding and deciphering centre located in England, was instrumental in the breaking and deciphering of the German Enigma messages. (RJP)

A German Enigma code machine. Throughout all of the Second World War the Germans believed their Enigma device to be impenetrable to deciphering. This, secret of the secrets, was also carefully guarded and maintained by the Allies. (RJP)

Above: An inflatable fake tank being easily lifted and moved. This was part of General Patton's make-believe army supposedly preparing for the invasion – FUSAG. Phoney prop tanks, barracks and aircraft were all part of the deception to convince the Germans that the Allies were intent on invading at Calais. Patton would later command the potent and real US Third Army in the drive through Europe. (LOC)

Left: German Generals von Rundstedt (right) and Rommel were both convinced the Allied invasion would take place somewhere near the French port of Calais. The FUSAG ruse helped maintain this deception. (Bundesarchiv)

Chapter 5

German Defences

If we do not succeed in our mission to close the seas to the Allies, or in the first 48 hours to throw them back, their invasion will be successful.

German Field Marshal Erwin Rommel

German Field Marshal Erwin Rommel believed the battle for Hitler's Atlantic Wall and the defeat of the Allied invasion was going to be won or lost on the beaches. In the early nineteenth century, the English Channel had prevented Napoleon Bonaparte from attempting to conquer and invade England. A century and a half later, the Channel kept Hitler and the Germans from invading and possibly conquering Great Britain. In accordance with this, Rommel recognised that the English Channel was his first and best line of defence. Rommel stressed that defensive preparations should concentrate on keeping the Allies in the water, by driving them off the beaches. The single aim of the Germans should be to push the Allies back into the surf and prevent them from establishing a beachhead. A successful beach landing would allow the Allies to reinforce in depth and then to mass their formidable forces. Rommel concluded that if the Allies were to solidly secure a beachhead position, then the battle, and the war, would be lost. It would then only be a matter of time until the stronger and logistically superior Allied forces drove the Germans back into Germany – and to the inevitable surrender.

Therefore, maintaining control of the beaches and keeping the assaulting army stranded in the water should be the primary task of all defensive thinking, as it was the only guarantee to prevent defeat. Rommel had been quoted as emphasising the importance of the beach defence and expressing the opinion: 'The first twenty-four hours of the invasion will be decisive … the fate of Germany depends on the outcome. For the Allies as well as Germany, it will be the longest day.'[5] It was a prophetic conclusion.

To oppose and thwart an Allied invasion, Hitler selected Rommel to strengthen his Fortress Europe's 'Atlantic Wall'. Assuming command in December of 1943, Rommel began examining where the invasion might fall, how to defend those positions, and constructing as rapidly as possible the means to blunt such an attack. Rommel soon began installing tens of thousands of obstacles, both steel and wood, to prevent landing craft from getting through the surf and onto the beaches. The steel obstacles would lie over 100 yards within the low tide point and prevent landing craft from nearing the inner beach area. Wooden poles would then be planted at angles and sunk close to the seawall to present the same problem to any landing craft able to negotiate closer in toward the shore. These obstacles were trimmed with a variety of explosive devices and anti-personnel and anti-vehicle mines (tank and landing craft). Several million mines were planted along the French coast.

The entrance to the beaches and the waters of the English Channel were strewn with anti-ship mines of all types: contact mines that detonated when struck by any vessel; magnetic mines that detonated when sensing the presence of a steel ship; and concussion/pressure mines that reacted to certain motions of water created by the movement of a ship. Rommel had already tripled the number of mines on the beach coasts and was hurriedly planting and laying hundreds of thousands more. The beach itself was peppered with buried mines laid in paths leading to the obviously predictable objectives of an invading column of vehicles or soldiers. Slowing and funnelling assaulting soldiers and vehicles would allow firing zones to be calculated and pre-sighted for machine-gun and artillery fire. The plan was to cause confusion and chaos and clog the beach entrances, while destroying as many assaulting soldiers and vehicles as possible from the protection of well-placed bunkers and pillboxes. On Omaha Beach alone, over 3,700 steel and wooden obstacles awaited the Allied landing craft. Omaha had been scheduled for further reinforcement, yet it already had the highest density of obstacles of any of the five Normandy beaches.[6]

Added to Rommel's vigorous defensive schemes and designs were other facts and figures that contributed to the selection of his tactics. A realist, Rommel understood that he would have little to no air support. By June 1944, the Allies outnumbered the Germans in aircraft by over 100 to 1, and on D-Day the Allies were able to place into the sky over 9,500 airplanes of all makes and sizes against a total German contingent of roughly less than 900.[7] An incredible disparity of force! Rommel, therefore, concentrated on the fixed defences, which included concrete and steel reinforced bunkers, pillboxes and heavy gun emplacements. Behind the seawall of a beach would be bands of barbed and concertina wire. Previously, all local buildings near to a Channel-fronting ridge or bluff, such as civilian dwellings, beach houses and boat sheds, had been destroyed to reduce any and all cover for the assaulting soldiers. Those sturdier buildings that remained were converted into machine-gun nests and artillery shelters.

British General Bernard Montgomery, overall commander of Eisenhower's ground forces, had fought against Rommel's army in the North African campaign and felt he had a good handle on Rommel's methods and intentions for defence. Montgomery commented, 'Rommel is an energetic and determined commander; he has made a world of difference since he took over [the Atlantic Wall defences] … He will do his best to not fight the armoured battle on the ground … but to avoid it altogether by using his tanks well forward … It is now clear that his intention is to deny us any penetration: Overlord is to be defeated on the beaches.'[8]

Rommel had debated with Hitler and other high-command generals on coastal tactics, leading to a compromised three-pronged division of ground units to defend the more than 500 miles of oceanic coastline. Rommel was given command of three mobile Panzer divisions that he kept close to the coast; his counterpart, General Leo Geyr von

Sweppenburg, was also given three mobile Panzer divisions to be placed in tactical reserve. Von Sweppenburg believed, and correctly as it turned out, that the Allies could not be stopped on the beaches but only through a fierce and concentrated counterattack. Rommel feared, also correctly, that the reinforcing units would not be able to arrive in time to alter the invasion. Rommel argued that any counterattacking reinforcement units would be severely hampered, if not destroyed, by the superior Allied air power – therefore, to be of value they must be kept close to where they were to be engaged. Finally, Hitler himself retained four divisions in strategic reserve, to be summoned when it was conclusively identified where the invasion was taking place and when to apply the necessary counterstroke. It was not what Rommel desired, but it was what he was forced to accept.

Rommel himself was a firm believer in the Pas de Calais as the location for the invasion and that region continued to get the lion's share of material and resources. But it remained a strategic mystery and a tactical uncertainty. Big guns, concrete bunkers and pillboxes rimmed the Pas de Calais and held the bulk of the fighting units. Rommel, however, increased the defences of the entire Atlantic coast and spent much personal effort strengthening, visiting and inspecting the fighting units that would engage the invading Allies on the beaches. Both Rommel and Montgomery foresaw a difficult and bitter battle upon landing; halting the Allies in the water and on the beaches would not be enough – a struggle would ensue. Omaha Beach would prove that point.

The Germans recognised that the Omaha Beach sector possessed significant transportation value for an invading army and its defences were developed on this basis. The frontal tidal beach defences were so designed as to prevent the Allies from ever gaining control of the beach, forcing the assault troops to cross hundreds of yards of mine and obstacle-strewn beach in order to reach and climb up the steep 100-foot bluff lining the beach proper. The entire Omaha Beach crescent presented a flat and mainly level sandy terrain possessing five gaps, or 'draws', that led off the beach shelf and into the countryside. It was these five 'draws' that the Allies sought to exploit and where the Germans craftily positioned their defences. By concentrating their defensive alignment, German firepower could dominate these five 'draws' and the movement of any Allied invaders, including their armoured vehicles. Concrete bunkers would house self-supporting artillery and machine-gun positions, providing enfilading fire across the beach and into the 'draws'. Where the defensive arc cresting the beach had received inadequate time or resources for formal bunkers and pillboxes, the defensive position utilised slit trenches that lined the bluffs overlooking the beach. If the Allies chose the Omaha region then Rommel's defences were projected to employ the access roads leading off of the beach and into the French interior as clearly identifiable firing zones. The Allies would seek to get off the beach as soon as possible and into the countryside, but in Rommel's defensive design, attackers would then be funnelled into these clearly pre-determined areas of slaughter.

Rommel understood the value of Omaha Beach and invested much of his resources and energy in fixed positions to ensure mutually assisting gunfire, from all angles and from all sizes of weaponry. Getting past the beach obstacles and minefields would expose any invaders to crossfire from both ends of Omaha's prominent flanking cliffs. Where time had permitted, tunnels and underground storage areas had been prepared, along with connecting trenches. Along the high bluffs overlooking the beach were machine-gun nests, pillboxes and fully reinforced concrete bunkers. The entire bluff and flanking cliffs enjoyed clear views of the beach, with all of the sightlines having been pre-marked and calculated for aim and accuracy. It was a 5-mile-long killing zone that threatened any intruder with an assortment of devastating crossfire.

Into many of these gun emplacements, Rommel placed the notorious 88 millimetre multi-purpose flak gun that doubled as a lethal tank destroyer. Dozens of mortars and machine guns and a few 75 millimetre all-purpose artillery pieces were also available to dissolve an attack. The flanking cliff bunkers were so well constructed that they were almost impervious to even a direct hit from naval gunfire or air bombs. A reporter from *The New Yorker* toured Omaha Beach several days after the landing and noted: 'The trenches were deep, narrow, and so convoluted that an attacking force at any point could be fired on from several directions … command post and mortar emplacements, were of concrete. The command post was sunk at least twenty-five feet into the ground and was faced with brick on the inside. The garrison had slept in underground bombproofs.'

Rommel and the Germans were clearly going to roll the dice in defeating the Allies on the beach – but the problem of which beach in France, and when, always remained. Due to Hitler's overzealous desire for conquest on multiple fronts, there was now for Rommel and the Germans too little time, too few resources and far too much beach. Such was the situation and the defensive fortifications awaiting the Allied invasion on Omaha Beach.

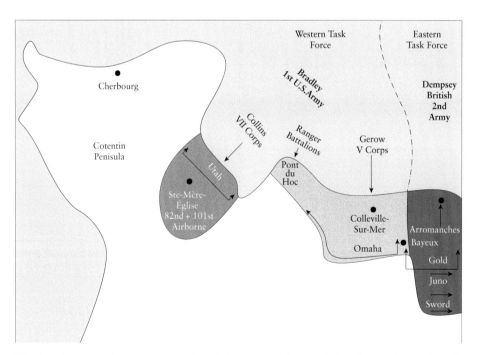

The American assault teams were assigned the western Normandy beaches, codenamed Utah and Omaha.

Thousands of these steel 'hedgehog' obstacles were placed along the French beaches above and below the tideline to impede landing craft. (RJP)

The Germans constructed hundreds of these concrete gun emplacements along the French coast. These bunkers housed barracks and troop facilities. (NARA)

The dreaded and potent German 88 mm flak gun proved to be an excellent anti-tank gun and was much respected by the Allies. This notorious weapon was a devastating combination of mobility and firepower and was a mainstay of any German military operation. (RJP)

A German soldier with what is probably an MG 42 machine gun. German defenders in France consisted of a very mixed lot: very young and very old recruits, recovering wounded, volunteer POWs from the Eastern Front and some crack Panzer units on refits. (LOC)

A pair of 105 mm naval guns used along the French coast to defend against Allied ships and landing craft. (RJP)

German Jagdpanzer IV armoured tank destroyer equipped with a 7.5 cm main gun. (RJP)

Thousands of these tetrahedral concrete beach obstacles peppered the French shoreline to impede landing craft. Many were topped with mines. (RJP)

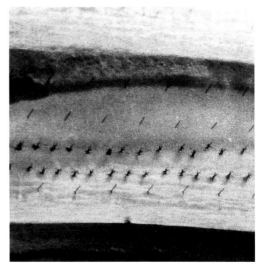

Above left: Thousands of these timber pole obstacles, many equipped with mines, littered the French beaches and were effective at both low and high sea levels. (NARA))

Above right: An aerial view of the German beach obstacles along the French coast. (NARA)

Above: German soldiers erecting timber pole beach obstacles along the French coast. (NARA)

Left: German Teller mines mounted on beach obstacles. (NARA)

A German concrete bunker at Longues-sur-Mer. Shell damage is clearly visible on the upper casement. A few of these bunkers retain their Second World War weapons. This nearly intact battery lies just east of Omaha Beach. (RJP)

Barracks and observation posts overlooking the cliffs of the Pont du Hoc. Some were impervious to aerial and naval bombardment. The heavily fortified bunkers were repeatedly bombed, but the commanding position remained a deep concern to American planners. (RJP)

Gun emplacement bunker at Pont du Hoc. It was found to be empty of big guns when seized by the US Army Rangers on D-Day. (RJP)

Chapter 6

Overlord Equipment

The sad state of war, has made it my duty to build.
Andrew Higgins, builder of the 'Higgins' landing craft that ferried thousands of amphibious soldiers on to the beaches of the European and Pacific theatres.

By definition, an amphibious landing would require the transfer of soldiers from ships to a shore or beach. Large transports would carry 150,000 Allied soldiers from their English ports of embarkation and then ferry them on smaller boats to the shore. It was a perilous operation in the best of conditions, let alone under enemy gunfire. The English Channel is often beset by storms and treacherous currents; crossing it at any time can induce seasickness even in large seaworthy ships. Depending upon their point of embarkation, the armada of amphibious transports would cross between 50 and 100 miles of mine-infested English Channel to reach Normandy. Several miles from the Normandy coast, the troops would offload onto smaller landing craft of various sizes and types for a perilous ride through the storm-tossed surf. If not already ill, most would now become seasick as they awaited their fate to land on the five D-Day beaches. With the troops would also come larger landing craft carrying a wide array of armoured vehicles, equipment, weapons and ammunition. Some armoured vehicles were designed to plough through the surf under their own power and navigation. Many would fail to negotiate the journey and swamp, drowning their crew before firing a shot or even being shot at. Such were the hazards and challenges of amphibious operations.

The Germans could not be engaged and defeated in Western Europe until assaulting troops were ferried safely and securely to the French coast. A few of these smaller landing vessels, all with odd acronyms and nicknames, became the primary method for delivering an army of soldiers from transport to shore. To meet this requirement, a variety of landing craft were designed and built, some subsequently being produced in extraordinary numbers. However, the need for ever more landing craft of all sizes remained a constant concern to the Overlord planners.

First and foremost was the 'Higgins' boat, the most widely built and often-used landing craft of any type. It was attached to a large transport and then loaded with soldiers for the journey to the beach. Besides personnel, it could also carry equipment, smaller vehicles, heavy weapons, or a combination of these things. Designed by Andrew Higgins, it was adaptable and ubiquitous. Usually labelled 'LCVP' (Landing Craft, Vehicles and Personnel), the Higgins boat was an inexpensive, self-propelled craft with a bow ramp for rapid unloading that dropped forward to discharge its load of men and equipment. The American version was made of wood, the British version of steel, and both models were used during D-Day. Of the more than 1,000 LCVPs the US Navy had available for D-Day, almost 100 were sunk, more than half of them on Omaha Beach alone.

Andrew Higgins had worked in the lumber business and had developed a method of forming wood into waterproof surfaces that could then be crafted into powerful lightweight landing boats for the war effort. His boatbuilding company was set up in 1940 in New Orleans, Louisiana, and began operation in anticipation of the need for such craft in the Second World War. His company eventually began assembling 700 landing boats a month to meet the enormous demand for amphibious landing craft. During the war, Higgins' company delivered over 20,000 landing craft. They were of three main types: the initial model, or LCP (Landing Craft Personnel), which could carry thirty-six soldiers; the larger version, the LCVP, which could carry thirty-six soldiers plus 5 tons of cargo or a small vehicle; and an even larger model, the LCM (Landing Craft Mechanised) that could handle 120 men, a medium tank or up to 30 tons of assorted equipment. His company also provided the wooden hulls for the US Navy's fast and versatile PT boats. Without these landing craft, the major amphibious landings against the Japanese-held Pacific islands, the Mediterranean landings, and of course D-Day, would have been problematic if not impossible.

There were many other important vessels for the off-loading of vehicles and personnel onto the shores of active war zones, including the essential Landing Ship Tank. The LST was a huge, flat-bottomed vessel with enormous twin doors in its bow, designed to carry several large vehicles such as tanks and trucks, hence the name. LSTs were longer than a football field at over 300 ft in length and, although slow-moving at barely 10 knots, they could literally drive right up and onto a beach to disgorge heavy armour and vehicles directly onto newly captured beaches. These shallow-draft, double-floored behemoths could operate without proper ports by beaching their bow and opening their huge frontal doors to drop a ramp and begin unloading nearly three dozen trucks, or nearly two dozen medium tanks. Used all over the Pacific and Atlantic theatres of war, more than 250 LSTs were employed at Normandy, delivering everything from tanks and jeeps to heavy equipment. On withdrawal, they could then be used to carry wounded soldiers back across the English Channel. Their size, lack of speed and valuable cargo made them a vulnerable and plum target, particularly for attacking warplanes, and several LSTs were sunk or damaged during the Overlord campaign.

Until an LST could safely unload a couple of dozen tanks at one time, the assaulting troops would need to rely on amphibious vehicles. The amphibious tanks and vehicles were of several designs, but all sought to accomplish the same thing: get high-powered armour and mobile weapons onto the beaches as soon as possible. It was a difficult challenge, and unfortunately for many of the D-Day crews, a deadly dangerous one too. The inability to get tanks ashore early and in quantity also resulted in complications for the freshly landed soldiers, who were in desperate need of armoured support as they confronted the German defenders. On Omaha Beach, where the greatest difficulties occurred, it proved to exacerbate a situation that was already bordering on failure and edging toward disaster.

Allied commanders counted on a certain number of armoured vehicles, such as tanks and anti-tank destroyers, surviving the distance between the transport vessels and the shore. On four of the five beaches, a sufficient number achieved this goal. On Omaha they did not. This was a dangerous journey for the heavy vehicles, as they were not designed to be amphibious. Numerous ideas were tested in order to provide this extremely important function of providing immediate armoured support and armoured protection for those troops crawling up the beach. This factor would be crucial to the success of engaging the dug-in German defenders.

Many schemes and ideas were literally floated for trial and experiment, including a skirt-like floatation device to keep out the surf while auxiliary propellers, powered by the tank's specially adapted 'Duplex-Drive' motor system, propelled the tank through the water. These tanks were then labelled as 'DD' for 'Duplex-Drive'. This DD amphibious version of the Sherman medium tank was developed to motor an armoured tank to the beach without being ferried by a landing craft. This would be particularly useful if these armoured vehicles could go in with the first group of assault units and provide both protection and firepower right from the earliest and most critical moments of the assaults.

Another form of independently arriving armoured vehicle was the 'wading tank' version of the Sherman tank. This format needed to be dropped off in shallow water, could fire its cannon from this position and would then track its way onto the beach proper. It had been used by the army during both the Sicily and Salerno invasions and was the preferred amphibious armoured vehicle of numerous American commanding officers at Normandy who feared that the DD tanks would not survive the surf and waves of the Omaha Beach conditions. Two tank battalions were included in the Omaha landings with a mix of the two amphibious types; two companies of DDs were to go in with the first wave, and one company of the 'wading trunk' types would go in later with the second wave.

At Omaha Beach, the first wave of armour was overwhelmed. The strong currents caused most of the armoured vehicles to be tragically washed over and under the rough surf, to founder and sink, while others were immobilised by equipment failure. Those remaining risked being destroyed by German gunfire even when successful in reaching the beach. The 16th Ranger Combat Team (RCT) was to be escorted by the 741st Tank Battalion, but only five of the thirty-two amphibious tanks assigned were able to successfully reach shore to back up the combat and engineer groups. The lack of immediate and adequately landed amphibious armour on Omaha

Beach had serious consequences for the infantry soldiers' ability to negotiate their movement from the drop point to the quasi-protective shelf of seawall beneath the main German gun pits and bunkers. Worse was the lack of armoured firepower to confront the fortified and elevated German defensive positions. It therefore required courageous action on the part of individual teams of infantry to eliminate and subdue the lethal German strong points with little or no armoured support. The other four invasion beaches, for a variety of reasons, enjoyed greater success in the delivery of their armoured units, which therefore contributed to lower casualty rates than those sustained by the unescorted units at Omaha.

'Hobart's Funnies' was the term used for an assortment of armoured vehicles devised to survive the journey through the surf and onto the Normandy beaches in order to clear and improve beach passage conditions. British Major General Percy Hobart was a tank officer in charge of organising and training British tank divisions, but he was called upon to use his imagination and expertise with tanks to produce a means to deliver them in these unique and hazardous circumstances. Numerous ideas, methods, and experiments were conducted, with the result being a variety of flotation devices and 'gadget vehicles'. These 'Funnies' were designed for specific invasion tasks and were built onto otherwise traditional armoured frames. One successful example involved using American Sherman 'crab' tanks equipped with a revolving drum of flailing front-end chains that whipped the ground, removing and discharging buried land mines or fence-mounted mines and barbed wire, thus clearing a path for following troops and vehicles. Others were British Churchill tanks equipped with diabolical long-range flamethrowers, as well as utility tanks carrying coiled steel fencing for either the laying of bridge work over culverts and ditches, or to lay stiffer roadway on the beaches themselves. All of these proved practical and useful.

One of the criticisms of the American command team, and General Bradley in particular, was their reluctance to accept advice on amphibious landings – advice from both British officers with their peculiar 'Funnies', and American officers from the Pacific theatre who had prior experience with amphibious vehicles and operations against sandy beaches defended by fanatically dedicated and well-equipped Japanese soldiers. Bradley and his cohorts felt that the beaches of France were physically different and that the operational scale was much larger. The response to the British 'Funnies' was the implied suggestion that these vehicles were gadgets that did not merit further discussion or development. Pacific commanders also recommended the use of armoured amphibious motorised vehicles (AMTRACS) to carry men and equipment ashore because they were more seaworthy in rough water and able to move both in water and on sandy beaches. Chief of Staff General George Marshall had sent several veteran American Pacific commanders, both Army and Marine, to assist the Normandy invasion, but their expertise and experience were generally dismissed.

The British tested many odd and creative ideas for landing craft and were willing to experiment to a greater degree than the Americans. This reluctance changed when, later in the campaign, the US Army encountered the difficult Bocage hedgerows within the interior of the Normandy countryside. American GIs would take it upon themselves to equip their Sherman tanks with former German steel beach obstacles and jerry-rig Bocage-penetrating fork-like prongs extending from the front of their Sherman tanks. It was an effective and efficient innovation. Unfortunately, the soldiers landing on Omaha were unable to adapt their vehicles to the immediate circumstances and were doomed to suffer the tragic consequences of shortcomings in their beach landing equipment.

SUPPLY

Obviously, the need for port facilities was vital. Feeding, arming, maintaining and reinforcing what would soon be a 500,000-man army would take fantastic amounts of supplies. Cargo crossing the English Channel in transports would be stymied unless the ships had immediate access to a pier, dock or harbour in which to unload. LSTs could only carry so much. What the Allied effort demanded was a deep-water port that could handle ocean-going freighters and transports to supply their titanic war effort. Since any European port seized would undoubtedly have been destroyed by retreating or surrendering Germans, an alternative was sought and devised. To sustain the initial 150,000 assault troops securing their Normandy beachhead and the thousands of reinforcements rapidly arriving to consolidate the position, plus the anticipated breakout into the interior of France, a port of some kind would be demanded. It would be two weeks before the port of Cherbourg would be captured and it would take over two months to repair after the Germans destroyed its facilities. The temporary answer would be the use of 'Mulberries'.

Mulberries were mammoth portable floating docks that were ferried across the English Channel to be linked together near shore in order to provide a deep-water docking platform for transport ships unloading troops, vehicles and supplies. Backed by the staunch support of British Prime Minister Winston Churchill, the 600-ton floating prefabricated concrete shells were the main means to unload larger ships until a full-scale port could be captured and repaired for full-time operation. Two of the Mulberry harbours were placed, one at Arromanches off the British Gold Beach, and an American one off Omaha Beach. The American Mulberry was destroyed by a ferocious Atlantic storm shortly after its installation. 200 LSTs provided temporary landing capacity. Hopelessly damaged, the American Mulberry was never repaired. The British Mulberry survived the storm and became essential. It was virtually the only docking facility on the Normandy coast until late July 1944, when the port of Cherbourg was sufficiently repaired and available for limited operation. A line of obsolete vessels was purposely sunk around the Mulberries to provide a protective breakwater. Ingeniously designed floating roadways that would rise and fall with the tide were then constructed to connect the Mulberry unit with the beach. The Mulberry engineer teams began work almost immediately on D-Day+2 of the invasion and soon formed a harbour 2 miles long and 1 mile wide, with enough docking space to handle up to seven supply ships at one time. Half a million troops, hundreds of tons of equipment and supplies and 80,000 vehicles were offloaded via the Mulberry harbour. Remnants of the Mulberry units and the adjoining breakwater hulks can still be seen offshore at Arromanches to this day.

For the actual fighting on the beach, dozens of specialty weapons were employed, one of the most common and effective being the 'Bangalore torpedo'. Bangalore torpedoes were long tubes filled with explosives and used to remove obstacles and barbed wire. Their length could be extended by connecting numerous pipe-like extensions and sliding the completed tube under or near the object to be blasted, where a long fuse would then detonate the business end. They were used frequently on the D-Day beaches by soldiers who were otherwise pinned down by gunfire.

Flamethrowers were used extensively and effectively to root out defenders hidden in bunkers, but the first arriving assault troops carrying these lethal and highly flammable fluid-laden devices were extremely vulnerable when attempting to struggle their way onto a tightly held beach or position. Armoured vehicles, including tanks, with long-range flame-throwing capability would have a devastating effect as the troops moved inland through the Bocage of interior rural France.

These incredibly inventive and invaluable devices were used to forward the military operation of Overlord.

Today on display at Arromanches are some of the sections of the floating roadways that connected the Mulberry ports to the shore. (RJP)

A heavy British Churchill tank. This being a Hobart 'Funny' model, a 'Crocodile', it ejected lethal flames from an especially adapted nozzle. (RJP)

A Higgins boat. Thousands of these landing craft in numerous variations provided the means to land soldiers, vehicles and weapons onto target beaches. (RJP)

Off the Normandy coast at Arromanches, the remains of the massive concrete Mulberry units that were floated across the English Channel to provide a makeshift portable harbour for the Normandy operation can still be seen. (RJP)

Bits and pieces of the Mulberry harbours still litter the beach and surf at Arromanches. (RJP)

The M-4 Sherman tank, produced in huge numbers by US factories throughout the war and used by all of the Allied forces. It normally mounted a 75 mm main gun, a 50 cal. heavy machine gun, a pair of 30 cal. machine guns and a crew of five. Later models had a heavier main weapon. (RJP)

An American M-10 tank destroyer. Using a basic M-4 Sherman tank carriage, it usually featured a 3-inch main gun mounted on a turret and a 50 cal. machine gun. (RJP)

One of many LSTs that provided immediate reinforcements of armour, equipment and supplies. These mammoth flat-bottomed vessels literally beached themselves to open their huge front doors. (NARA)

One of Hobart's Funnies, a flail tank to destroy mines and barbed wire. These were among the numerous imaginative devices that contributed to the success of the Normandy operation. (LOC)

Yankee ingenuity. American soldiers devised fork-like iron prongs attached to their tanks in order to penetrate the bushy French Bocage. (LOC)

The Mulberry portable dock and roadway at the British Sword Beach. The American Mulberry at Omaha was destroyed by the 'Great Storm' of 19–21 June. (US Navy)

Mulberry Harbour. An aerial view of the breakwater and portable Mulberry dock with numerous transport ships waiting to unload and supply the budding 500,000 man army required for the coming battle of Normandy. (US Navy)

Mulberry Harbour and floating roadway leading to the beach proper. (US Navy)

Chapter 7

Overlord Air Power

The railway network is completely wrecked … local and through traffic is impossible … it is useless to attempt further repair work.

German report of June 1944 prior to D-Day due to the results of the Allied 'Transportation Plan' to eliminate both the German air force and means to adequately reinforce Normandy.

So strong was the Allied air superiority on D-Day that not one single plane was shot down by German aircraft. Although 113 Allied planes were brought down by enemy anti-aircraft fire, none of the damage was done by the Luftwaffe, which was unable to mount any type of defence.[9] In fact, Germany had virtually no air force remaining. On D-Day alone, the Allies employed 3,000 heavy bombers, 1,500 medium bombers and over 5,000 fighters to combat an almost empty catalogue of German combat aircraft.[10] Allied planes delivered pulverising ground support to the five invasion beaches, knocking out bunkers, pillboxes, slit trench defences and encased gun revetments. More importantly, however, was the tactical support attacking roads, railways and junctions behind the enemy lines that prevented any movement of German mobile reinforcement. The dreaded and feared Panzer armour divisions never left their stand-to positions, believing all along that the Allied attack at Normandy was only a feint and that the real attack was to come elsewhere, probably at the Pas de Calais. Assuming the mobile Panzer armoured divisions had ventured into action, it is more than conceivable that they would have been decimated by the tactical air arm of the Allies. As it was, they remained in reserve to fight another day.

As dominant as the Allied air weapon was on D-Day, the real work of the air command had been accomplished months in advance. Priority had been given to Eisenhower and the SHAEF commanders. They exercised full operational advantage to continue the ruse of the Calais point of attack while hiding the intended Normandy location, as well as obliterating every access road and rail line that could provide any support for the coastal defences. The ratio was two to one, with Normandy back lines receiving the 'one', as compared to the other 'two' going to additional potential targets, including Calais. Even with this diminished ratio, no road or rail junction or staging area would be neglected for repeated pounding by the air forces. So thorough were air raids that by late May 1944, very few targets remained, and very little traffic could safely move in daylight on the open road or rail routes as it had become near-suicidal. So too had the German Luftwaffe been destroyed: either on the ground, or drawn into the air for combat. By late spring 1944, the skies had been cleared of German warplanes and there was no thought of replacing either the planes or the crews. In fact, the veteran aircrews had been destroyed before the replacement aircraft became available. The only remaining pilots and crews were fresh, green replacements with little or no experience. Hopelessly outnumbered and inexperienced, these raw recruits were easy pickings for the Allied air command.

When D-Day arrived, the Allies controlled the skies and dominated the roads, rails and junction depots over France. Unfortunately, a difficult decision had to be made early in 1944 when the invasion air assault began in earnest: what about the French civilians? The answer was to accept the consequences in order to gain the essential triumph. As it turned out, French civilians suffered over 15,000 casualties in and around the German transport and staging areas. Such was the cost inflicted on friend and foe alike for the liberation of Nazi-occupied France. Indeed, so concerned were the Allies about the threat of casualties to the French civilian population that, prior to the preliminary bombing campaign leading up to D-Day, millions of leaflets were dropped, defining and explaining the necessity for the bombing of French civilian targets. Beginning in March 1944, 130 million were distributed from Allied aircraft flying over France, and thereafter over 100 million each month leading up to D-Day. It was a legitimate fear since, during the entire war, Allied bombing missions over France killed more than 53,000 French civilians while injuring at least 70,000 more. This compares to over 40,000 British civilians killed during the German Blitz of 1940–41, and perhaps as many as 60,000 Britons for the entire war.[11] Certainly the massive pre-invasion bombing campaign was required, and just as certainly there were going to be French civilian casualties. The issue was debated in the highest SHAEF circles, but in March 1944, Eisenhower came down firmly with the decision to use heavy and continuous bombing raids on the rail system, marshalling yards and any and all strategic targets before and during the invasion of France.[12] There would, of course, also be collateral damage and casualties due to bad weather, mission error and the locations of the targets in urban areas, but that risk too would have to be accepted.

The level of French civilian casualties that could be tolerated and the ensuing political ramifications with an ally were also debated, but again, the decision hinged on the goals of completely bottling up the capacity for German reinforcement before, during and after the invasion. For the six-month campaign, seventy-six key locations were identified on the French railway network alone. Civilian casualty estimates ranged from RAF Bomber Command's prediction of 80,000–160,000 French casualties to a survey conducted by British scientific advisor Solly Zuckerman that suggested 12,000 would be killed and 6,000 more seriously injured.[13]

Zuckerman and Eisenhower's Chief of Allied Expeditionary Air Force for the invasion, Trafford Leigh-Mallory, had developed what was known as the

'Transportation Plan' to substantially reduce the reinforcing German units by completely destroying the rail system leading west of Paris. While potentially effective in every aspect of tactical design, it threatened large numbers of French civilians. Prime Minister Winston Churchill had deep reservations about the campaign but reluctantly gave his approval due to the necessity of the action and the need to do everything to ensure the overall success of the invasion. The casualty figures were recorded and reported by French resistance fighters, and through the month of April 1944 the rate of 1,000 dead per month was in line with the more conservative predictions. However, by May 1944 it was clear that a more concentrated level of bombardment would be required, and at Roosevelt's insistence, Churchill gave his final approval and the unrestricted campaign assumed a more pronounced focus.

The preliminary bombing campaign then began in earnest as over 63,000 tons of bombs were dropped on French transportation targets alone.[14] But of course, much of this explosive power was off the mark and nowhere near any pre-determined targets. The result effectively devastated German transport of supplies, reinforcements and equipment, but it was also costly in French civilian casualties: from 700 killed in March to 5,000 in April, and then a leap to 9,800 and 9,500 in May and June respectively. This meant over 25,000 killed during the six months leading up to the invasion – or more than double the conservative estimates.

There were other disputes concerning the use of air power. Disagreements between the various air groups generated friction over the use of heavy bombers versus lighter and faster fighter-bombers, and a further argument between airmen and infantry officers as to the benefits of the air interdiction at all. Eisenhower was almost powerless to resolve the disputes and called upon Marshall in Washington to finally settle the question and place everyone on the same page – this being that the Overlord mission would hold precedent through the spring and until the invasion was completed.[15] Only partially successful through early spring, the turning point came when the decision was reached to use the overwhelming Allied strength of over 9,000 fighters in the fighter-bomber interdiction mode. Turned loose in late March, for the next two months the fighter-bombers of the US 9th Air Force did what had been exceedingly difficult for the high-altitude, heavy bombers to accomplish, even with their huge tonnage of saturation bombing. Particularly devastating was the destruction of railway repair sheds, preventing the repair of locomotives and rail carriages, and railway bridges over the rivers west of Paris that were nearly impossible for the higher-altitude heavies to hit but were extremely vulnerable to low-flying fighters such as the P-47 Thunderbolt. The havoc created by these tactics, coupled with the strafing of trains in movement, rail yards, junctions and staging areas, made train travel a nightmare for the Germans and certain death for anyone who attempted to travel by road or rail during the day. By D-Day, virtually no rail or road traffic by day was even being attempted, let alone succeeding. A secondary benefit was the continued annihilation of the German Luftwaffe, both on the ground and in the air, when feebly attempting to challenge the Allied interdiction program. In short, it became a stunning success.[16]

On D-Day, the Allies placed 10,000 aircraft over Europe with virtually no interference from the Luftwaffe. Even if the Allied chiefs were not in total agreement over method and means, there was no question as to the need and the strength of the air arm as it dominated the skies over the English Channel and all of western France. At Omaha, the bombing mission for the air forces was conducted in stages and in concert with the naval bombardment. The first phase of the air action used heavy bombers. The specifically defined targets were the bluffs rimming Omaha Beach, the heavily reinforced concrete bunkers, and the roads leading into the target areas. What was not attacked was the actual beach itself – this was to prevent the bombing action from severely cratering the beach and adding to the obstacles for the armoured units that were to gain access to the shore and penetrate beyond. This point had been debated by the commanders, who weighed the value of 'cover' bombing on the immediate objective – the beach – against leaving the beach clear for the oncoming armoured vehicles to pierce the German front line, and then for the necessary mass arrival of supply and reinforcement vehicles to follow. Controversial as it was, and after much discussion, it was decided to leave the actual beach area intact and concentrate the air attacks on the bluffs and beyond. This would prove faulty in action since the shoreline defences, in particular at Omaha Beach, were brimming with machine-gun pillboxes, concrete bunkers and slit trenches filled with defenders.

Another concern was collateral damage to the attacking forces. Weather dictated precision, and bad weather limited the degree of precision and greatly increased the risk of lethal Allied 'friendly fire'. Without the guarantee of clear weather, and considering the close proximity to the invading assault groups, there was fear that bombing and strafing too close to the attacking invaders would risk far too much danger and threat of lethal 'friendly fire'. The weather on D-Day was cloudy and, in this sense, the more conservative decision may have balanced out. However, there was no fall-back plan for the use of either heavy or medium bombers at low altitude under the cloud cover, and when the overcast skies interfered, the use of these weapons on the actual shore front was completely denied. Unlike the later Pacific island invasion operations, there was no available aircraft carrier support nor a communications network to call in tactical air strikes as needed. This use of combined naval, air, ground and communication networks was in its infancy, and was not featured in the Atlantic calculation. It would later advance and evolve in the extensively amphibious Pacific theatre.

At adjacent Utah Beach, the problem was met by medium bombers flying parallel to the coast to provide low-level support. At Omaha, the need was not served in any adequate manner and was underscored by the resistance of the undestroyed German defences. The question of using heavy bombers for tactical deployment had already led to bitter and continuous disputes throughout the Normandy campaign, and heavy bombers used in this mode were found to be wanting. Lack of sufficient training, the inaccuracy of the weapon systems for specific tactical targets as opposed to strategic area targets, and weather factors all limited the suitability of strategic heavy bombers to properly conduct tactical missions. This had been pointed out to Eisenhower and the Allied high command by both British and American air commanders, but they were overruled due to the necessity of complete commitment to the invasion's success. However, the larger and greater use of fighters and medium bombers proved more and more effective as the campaign developed, and they gradually became accepted as essential to the concept of mixed-weapons warfare. On Omaha Beach and the other four assault beaches, tactical air support from single-engine fighter planes was limited to providing air umbrella protection over the invading fleet and its vast array of ships, along with escort cover for the bombers operating deeper into France. It was to figure little in the actual invasion day battle. As the Normandy fighting continued over the next few months, however, the tactical air support, especially from lighter fighter aircraft, would improve and expand. This produced devastating effects on retreating German formations and, in particular, the violent rout of the retreating armies at the Falaise Pocket in late July 1944 as the Allies finally succeeded in breaking out of Normandy.

A British Spitfire fighter at a recent American air show. These and other Allied fighters provided umbrella air cover for the invasion on D-Day. (RJP)

An American B-17 heavy bomber at a recent American air show. It was part of the 'Transportation Plan' to destroy the French railway system prior to D-Day. (RJP)

The American P-47 Thunderbolt fighter was used for effective and devastating low-level interdiction of French rail lines and to provide umbrella air cover during D-Day. (US Army)

Seen at a recent American air show, this P-51 Mustang fighter was used to provide umbrella air cover over the D-Day landings. (RJP)

A-20 Havocs, typical medium bombers, over French rail yards while destroying and blocking German military transportation prior to D-Day. (NARA)

Devastation of French rail yards as carried out according to the controversial 'Transportation Plan' to disrupt German operations prior to D-Day. (NARA)

General Pete Quesada, commander of American fighter forces during Normandy campaign. It was Quesada who famously, and correctly, predicted that 'there would be no German Air Force' to oppose the Allies on D-Day. (US Army)

Churchill and Eisenhower generally got along well, occasional differences of opinion notwithstanding, and shared an excellent relationship. One major disagreement concerned the heavy bombing of French rail lines and rail yards preceding D-Day. Churchill feared a heavy toll of French civilian casualties, while the Overlord high command demanded completed severing of the German ability to reinforce Normandy. Roosevelt interceded and the Transportation Plan went ahead to great success, although so too did Churchill's feared civilian casualties. (US Army)

Chapter 8

Naval Bombardment

I am firmly convinced that our supporting naval fire got us in; that without the gunfire we positively could not have crossed the beaches.
                    Colonel Stanhope B. Mason, Chief of Staff, 1st Infantry Division

The preliminary American naval bombardment was conducted by two older battleships, USS *Arkansas* and USS *Texas*, several cruisers that included the French *Montcalm* and *Georges Leygues* and the British *Glasgow* and *Belona*, and fifteen destroyers. There were, of course, dozens of smaller ships, both transports and fighting craft. Behind the initial invading fleet was a huge armada of support and supply ships, eager and anxious to unload more troops, weapons and supplies once the beachhead was established. The naval flotilla crossing the English Channel to all five of the beaches, Operation Neptune, was under command of British Admiral Sir Bertram Ramsey. The American sector, which included the western beaches of Omaha and Utah, was under American Admiral Alan Kirk aboard the American cruiser USS *Augusta*. The Omaha Beach operations were being directed by US Admiral John Hall. The first naval barrage began at first light and attempted to silence the German gun emplacements along Omaha Beach and the nearby Pont du Hoc. This counter-battery fire was intended to mop up any remaining German artillery left undestroyed by the aerial bombing missions of the last few weeks and also to provide shell holes where the invading soldiers could take cover as they arrived on the beach. The air phase had been limited to smaller-sized bombs to prevent oversized craters on the beach from impeding arriving Allied tanks and armoured vehicles. Therefore, it was up to the big naval guns to provide the accurate reduction of targets deployed in heavily embedded concrete bunkers. This phase of naval bombardment lasted 30 minutes, until 06:30, when the landing craft began to arrive on the beaches. There were fourteen known German heavy gun positions of various size and strength, and these were laid on with the initial fire. The bombardment would fire both onto forward beach positions and those in depth, even if they had previously been ruled as out of action.

  At midnight on 6 June, the initial naval component of minesweepers sailed across the English Channel to begin sweeping the five coastal regions that would be used as the landing area for the transports and the 150,000 soldiers to be disembarked. The minesweepers had two important tasks: sweep the English Channel passages for the forthcoming transports, and clear areas nearer the beach to allow the gunboat units to operate. The minesweepers encountered no enemy activity and were able to complete their operation in time for the arrival of the warships that would commence the shore bombardment preceding the landings.

During the initial 30-minute bombardment, the barrage of naval explosives concentrated on the actual beach emplacements in an attempt to fully reduce and destroy most, if not all, of the embedded gun bunkers, any anti-tank guns, the dreaded German 88 mm guns and the remaining dug-in light machine-gun positions and pillboxes. Allied commanders had debated as to whether their goals would be better served by an extended bombardment for hours, or even days, as done in the Pacific with the Japanese-held islands. This option was eventually rejected in favour of a short hurricane bombardment, followed by an immediate launching of the landing craft in order to maintain the element of surprise.

Another component of the pre-landing bombardment was the use of vessels designed for the firing of multiple short-range rockets. These specialised craft could launch an avalanche of high explosives onto the beach ahead of the landing troops in a minimum amount of time. There were thirty-six of these 'LCT's, with each craft carrying over 1,000 rockets and able to toss 65,000 pounds of high explosives within 90 seconds to blanket a target. Eight of these LCTs were assigned to Omaha Beach and, though loud and spectacular, they were poorly aimed and shells mainly fell short of the beach, so they unfortunately had little to no effect.

As the landing craft left their transports and approached the beaches, the bombardment lifted from firing on the beach proper and began concentrating on the rear echelons and bluffs behind the beaches and flanks, destroying or pinning down any would-be reinforcement units. Admiral Hall, in particular, was not satisfied with either the allotment of time for effective heavy bombardment or the number of gunboats assigned to Omaha, feeling it was insufficient to completely silence the German gun positions. Hall also placed greater emphasis on the need for more destroyers, with their shallow draft to manoeuver close in to the beach and provide intense protective covering fire on any German gun emplacements that had not been previously knocked out. The deep-water bay leading into the beach proper was exceptionally useful and vital for the incoming temporary Mulberry piers being floated across the Channel, but it also allowed destroyers and other shallow drafted gunships to penetrate within 1,500 yards of the beach itself to supply supporting counter-fire for the assaulting troops.

Due to the tidal conditions of Omaha Beach, the assault needed to be earlier than any of the other beaches, and more significantly, it allowed for a shorter time span for the reduction of the German beach defences. This considerably altered the situation for the Omaha Beach assault, and contributed to the potential disaster that ensued there. Even more telling was the unfortunate number of German guns that had remained unscathed during the opening bombardments, wreaking havoc on the assaulting waves of arriving soldiers. Omaha Beach had been left short in pre-landing preparation, both in allotted time and weight of force, adding to its already being the deadliest and most difficult of the five beach landings. In short, the early morning big gun naval bombardment was too brief; the follow-up air bombardment that dropped 13,000 bombs was mainly off-target due to poor weather conditions, falling far to the rear on French countryside; and the spectacular massed use of rockets fell short of their beach targets. Later in the day, and at a critical juncture in the Omaha operation, the timely close-in contribution of the smaller destroyers and escorts would provide a salvation with their essential element of withering near point-blank firing against German gun pits and bunkers. Bravely operating in shallow waters and dangerously at risk of both running aground and enemy gunfire, the accurate and smothering covering gunfire vitally contributed to the eventual success of the attacking units struggling to overcome the determined German defences.

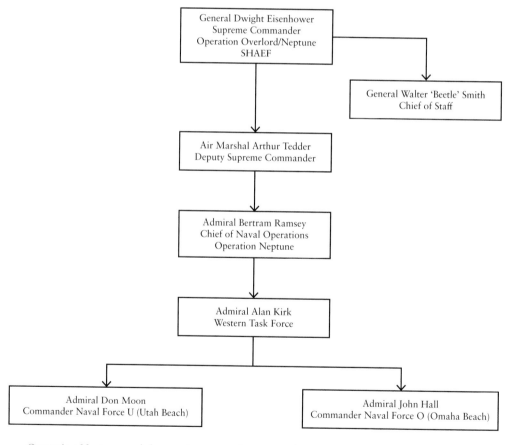

Operation Neptune and the naval command structure for crossing the English Channel and landing on the two western/American beaches, Utah and Omaha.

Above left: Admiral John Hall, commander of American naval forces for Omaha Beach on D-Day. Prior to D-Day, Hall had requested more destroyers for inshore support and more heavy naval bombardment prior to the landings. The destroyers would prove to be critically important to the eventual success at Omaha. (US Navy)

Above right: Big 14-inch guns from the battleship USS *Nevada* firing on nearby Utah Beach. (US Navy)

The battleship USS *Arkansas*. Her 12-inch main guns provided pre-invasion bombardment at Omaha Beach. (US Navy)

The battleship USS *Texas*. Its heavy 14-inch main guns provided powerful naval bombardment at Pont du Hoc. She has been preserved as a museum ship in Texas, at the San Jacinto Historical site. (RJP)

Chapter 9

Omaha Beach Assault Plan

Amphibious operations are among 'the most difficult in war'.
Nineteenth-century European military theorist Antoine-Henri Jomini

One other major determining factor would be the weather. Springtime storms along the English Channel are often violent and frequent, but most ominously they are unpredictable. The timetable for the Allied invasion hinged on a very limited number of calendar dates that offered the combination of certain tide heights, moonlit skies and – of course – favourable weather. The army desired high tides to skim over obstacles and have less beach to cross, the navy sought low tides to expose the obstacles for incoming landing craft and the air wing required moonlight to assist pilots in spotting observation points. A compromise was met; the invasion dates would have to incorporate moonlight and a landing craft release roughly three hours after low tide, and all with weather permitting. This meant few available dates and a gamble that the weather would not cause an extended postponement or, worse, the destruction of the assault fleet. As D-Day approached, the weather turned increasingly stormy. The early June weather and accompanying forecast was so inclement that German Field Marshal Erwin Rommel returned home to Germany to holiday with his family, so sure was he that the nasty weather would prevent any attempt of an invasion. 5 June, the original D-Day, was cancelled by Eisenhower on the advice of his meteorologists. His staff concurred. The weather was wretched.

The enormous enterprise now paused to await fair weather. Previous Allied assaults in North Africa, Sicily and the Pacific Islands had been much smaller in size, design and goal. At Normandy, the number of ships in the flotilla, the sheer size of the invading force and the 50-mile frontal area designated for the assault were all many times larger and potentially more formidable than any previous contemplated amphibious invasion. Operation Overlord would involve not only meticulous planning in every phase of the enterprise, but also a size commitment unparalleled in the history of warfare. But cooperation from Mother Nature would be required.

The Allies had conducted amphibious landings in Morocco and Algeria in Africa; Sicily, Salerno and Anzio in Italy; and the disastrous experimental 'practice' landing at Dieppe in France in 1942. The US had previous experience in the brutally violent island assaults in the Pacific. None of these, though, would approximate the magnitude and logistical preparation presented by the invasion of Europe. Sheer numbers alone of troops, ships, airplanes and supplies would dwarf all previous endeavours.

Numerous inventions, some successful and others less so, would be unveiled and unleashed. The floating Mulberry portable harbours; the 'Pluto' hose (a pipeline under the English Channel), carrying fuel directly across the English Channel to Normandy; and the chain-whipping tanks to remove landmines and barbed wire emplacements were just a few of the suggestions and inventions. There were scores of others in varying scope of feasibility or lunacy that had been suggested, tested and developed for this one single invasion. But the postponement from 5 June, and possibly beyond due to weather, could not be compensated for by invention or preparation. As William the Conqueror had waited for fair winds in 1066, so too did the Allies await a favourable forecast to embark across the Channel.

It was planned and conducted accordingly. The naval component to actually deliver the forces to the Normandy beaches, Operation Neptune, engaged the largest fleet ever assembled. The flotilla consisted of over 1,000 vessels: warships, landing craft and supply ships that would encompass 200,000 sailors and seamen, which outnumbered the ground forces involved. Granted, the distance being traversed was only 100 miles on average from ports such as Southampton, Portsmouth and Plymouth, but the treacherous and storm-wracked seas of the English Channel made any crossing, even in favourable weather, an extremely hazardous and dangerous undertaking. Added to that, it wasn't just an ordinary crossing of the Channel from port to port; it was to land a 150,000-man army on five beaches in unpredictable weather conditions, through dangerous minefields and under the gunfire of one of the most formidable armies on the European continent, indeed in all of history. Even after a successful landing, the Allies were to be confronted with a desperate German reaction and recovery. The British sought to quickly seize the junction city of Caen, near the eastern flank of the British-designated Sword Beach. So too was there optimism for a rapid breakout into the French countryside on the American western flank from Omaha and Utah beaches. But such was the unknown resistance awaiting the Allied ground forces as they finally hit the beaches on 6 June 1944 that getting ashore and holding position would be considered a triumph.

Part of the Omaha assault plan included a daring assault on the over 100-foot-high cliffs of adjacent Pont du Hoc, which overlooked both American beaches (Omaha and Utah). The prominent observation point possessed massive German guns and posed a serious threat to the American operation. This project was deemed essential to the overall Omaha Beach plan.

Omaha Beach itself is a sandy arc of roughly 10 kilometres (about 6 miles) with high cliffs on either end of the arc and a long ridge behind the beach of roughly 100 feet in height. Depending upon the tide, the ridgeline is between 100 and 400 yards away from the surf as it strikes the beach. Recognising the importance of this beach, the Germans had adequately prepared it with a lethal set of defensive systems to block Allied landing and penetration. It would be a tough nut for the Allies to crack.

The Allies would attempt to land on the beach, gain the bluff, eliminate the German gun emplacements, move up the gullies or 'draws' and pierce the rear area into the French countryside. This would have been a tall order under any circumstances, let alone arriving as an amphibious assault, under heavy gunfire and landing under difficult weather conditions.

The assault on Omaha Beach was assigned to 'task force groups' that would land and fight their way up the bluffs and on to their objective points. The initial combat units on Omaha Beach were composed of the Ranger Combat Teams (RCTs) and specially trained engineer units to clear the beaches, bluffs and surrounding areas of obstacles and mines. They would attempt to lay paths for the oncoming units arriving in successive waves. The overall combat divisions selected by General Omar Bradley included elements from the 1st Infantry Division (nicknamed the 'Big Red One' after the large red number '1' on their shoulder patches) and the 29th Division (nicknamed the 'Blue and the Gray' due to the two colours on their shoulder patches). The veteran 1st Division was hand-picked by Bradley as the most experienced of US units due to its action in the Mediterranean and Italy, and the 29th due to its strict and disciplined training programme while preparing in Britain. The 29th was unusual in that it was basically a National Guard division from Baltimore, Maryland, that had been beefed up and fleshed out with conscripts. It was to prove an effective fighting unit throughout the French campaign. Each division was also supported by a tank battalion for increased firepower.

The individual units spearheading the initial assault on Omaha Beach were composed of two regimental combat teams incorporating engineers and support groups. Specialised units were blended in with these assault groups in order to provide a mixed force combining utility, punch and firepower. Armoured vehicles were also included, and it was the failure to successfully land these early arriving armoured groups that led to much of the confusion and paralysis – and the near failure – of the entire Omaha operation.

Gap Assault Teams were assigned to blast 50-yard gaps through the beach obstacles and obstructions, enabling the follow-up landing teams and armour groups to have a path across the beach and up the bluffs. This was a vitally important component of the initial assault since it would open lanes for the reinforcing units of infantry and armour. Many of the RCT and engineer units involved in the actual landing possessed considerable experience and training from previous invasions of Tunisia, Sicily and Italy. They were hardened, well-trained and, in most instances, veterans. If successful, the following waves of troops and armour would pour through these seams and gaps and begin penetrating inland for the seizure of roads, junctions and outlet passages into the open space of Normandy. Such was the hope. However, these early escorting groups were practically obliterated on arrival and the openings were not available. To further complicate the situation, the accompanying armour foundered in the surf and those troops who landed and survived were therefore without armoured support. Chaos and confusion reigned, the assault plan collapsed into shambles and a disastrous failure loomed.

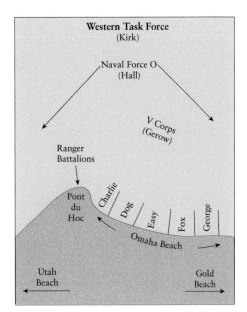

Omaha Beach in detail, plus the nearby Pont du Hoc. Omaha would prove to be the most difficult of the five Normandy beaches.

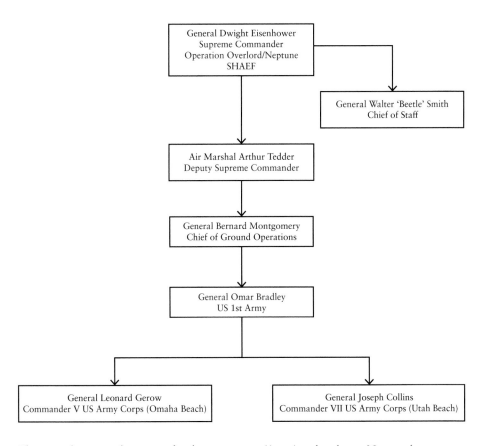

The ground command structure for the two western/American beaches at Normandy.

General Dwight Eisenhower with American airborne soldiers the day before D-Day. (US Army Signal Corps)

The broad, crescent-shaped shore of Omaha Beach with a clearly visible and stoutly embedded German bunker stuffed into the bluff on the right. This commanding position enabled the Germans to pour deadly fire onto soldiers and landing craft. (RJP)

American GIs aboard a transport vessel crossing the English Channel shortly before the D-Day landing. (US Navy)

Loading an American Sherman tank fitted with a wading attachment that would hopefully allow it to disembark in low ocean surf. (US Navy)

Omaha Beach, as viewed today from the overlooking bluffs. It was these commanding bluffs that gave the Germans such a strong defensive advantage at Omaha. (RJP)

A fully loaded American LST transport with heavy equipment and vehicles, crossing the English Channel to land on the Normandy beaches. (US Navy)

Chapter 10

D-Day: Pont du Hoc

'OK, we'll go'.
Allied Supreme Commander General Dwight Eisenhower to his staff on going ahead
with the invasion as a narrow window of favourable weather appeared for 6 June.

Atop the rocky point overlooking Omaha Beach stood the formidable cliffs and concrete bunkers of the big gun emplacements situated on Pont du Hoc. Taking place at the same time as the main Omaha landing and just to the south-west of the main Omaha Beach sector, a bold and separate landing was conducted using specialised US Ranger units to scale the 150-foot cliffs of Pont du Hoc and destroy the large German guns. It had been apparent from the first Omaha Beach planning that someone, somehow, was going to have to knock out the guns on Pont du Hoc. These fierce guns were a threat not only to ships along the Omaha and Utah Beaches, but to any transports approaching either of the beaches as well as to their disembarking assault landing craft. American General Omar Bradley felt it was absolutely imperative to have these guns silenced due to their threat to the Channel waters and both American beaches. This task was assigned to the specially trained 2nd and 5th Ranger Battalions under the command of Lieutenant Colonel James Rudder, as part of the 1st Division attacking Omaha Beach.

Reconnaissance photos indicated that large steel and concrete emplacements on the high cliffs of Pont du Hoc contained several 155 mm guns capable of firing to ranges of up to 15 miles into the English Channel. Dominating both Utah and Omaha beaches were six of these powerful guns, which were extremely well protected within fortified casements of steel and concrete. Bunkers protected their defending crews in equally hardened shelters. Even lacking the firepower of the big guns, the 'point' commanded a superb observation capacity to identify the approach and movements of an invasion force. The position had been designated for repeated air bombardment, but reconnaissance photos showed no discernible damage. It therefore became a high priority in the planning of the first day's assault. Specially prepared teams, using ladders, ropes and grappling hooks, received intense training to enable them to land on the beach beneath the cliffs, scale the 150-foot cliffs while under fire, seize the position and disarm the big guns. All of this was to be accomplished at the opening of the first day's initial assault. It was literally a tall order.

To increase the chances of success, the air wing had devastated the Pont du Hoc area for several weeks. Further insurance was provided by the delivery of a pulverising naval bombardment on the morning of the invasion from the battleship USS *Texas*. During the 30-minute pre-landing bombardment, the mighty 14-inch guns of the *Texas* would concentrate on reducing the heavily defended bunkers and reinforced concrete gun emplacements. Unbeknownst to intelligence, the German guns had been withdrawn and camouflaged in a nearby depot. Due to the stiff currents and ongoing confusion, the landing craft delivered their Ranger units more than 30 minutes later than scheduled. The 2nd Ranger Battalion was only able to land 220 assault climbers to fight their way up the cliffs, while the majority of the 5th Ranger Battalion ended up drifting even further east, landing on the actual Omaha Beach. In the face of intense German resistance, eighty determined Rangers under Lt-Col. Rudder were able to reach the summit and successfully overcome the defending units that occupied the area. Unbelievably, the gun emplacements were then discovered to be empty, or lined with wooden logs posing as guns! The Germans had decided to withdraw the guns and relocate them behind the exposed shoreline cliffs. However, the persistent Rangers were not to be denied their goal. They penetrated inland until they located the guns, hidden in a rear area, and proceeded to wreck them. By this point, they had suffered over 50 per cent casualties.

The fight for Pont du Hoc was not over, as it remained a valuable location for German observation and for any other guns the Germans might later reinstall. Therefore, the Rangers now sought to retain possession of their captured redoubt in the face of stiff German counter-attacks. With over half of their contingent strength killed or wounded, the remaining elements were ordered to fan out, look for German patrols and develop a defensive position. Messages were sent out for reinforcements, supplies and ammunition, but for a time this could not be carried out for lack of either effective communication or readily available resources. Later they were joined by members of the 5th Ranger Battalion and others from the 19th Infantry Division and, although completely isolated from the main invading force at Omaha Beach, managed to hold on to their position and eventually unite with the hopefully expanding US combat forces from Omaha Beach.

The steep, forbidding cliffs at Pont du Hoc. (RJP)

The American Rangers with their captured German prisoners at the recently seized position of Pont du Hoc. (US Army)

The German guns at Pont du Hoc had all been removed and hidden prior to the invasion. The determined American Rangers found the guns anyway and destroyed them while also seizing and holding the position. (RJP)

The cliffs at Pont du Hoc. This high-up position offered a commanding gun and observation advantage, hence the necessity for it to be taken on the first day of the invasion. (RJP)

Chapter 11

D-Day: Omaha Beach Invasion

We shall see who fights better and who dies more easily, the German ... [for] his homeland or the Americans and British, who don't even know what they are fighting for.
German General Alfred Jodl, chief of the German high command.

The great airborne assaults conducted by the United States Army's 82nd and 101st airborne divisions the night before D-Day took place at the south-western edge of the five invasion beaches and were used to secure the right or western flank of Utah Beach. So, too, were British airborne units dropping behind Sword Beach in order to secure the bridges, roads and eastern flank of the overall D-Day assault. The main landings at all five beaches followed only a few hours later.

Of the five beach invasions, Omaha was deemed the toughest and also possibly the most important. It would link with the American Utah Beach to the west and the central British Gold Beach to the east. Omaha would serve as cover for the Utah units to cut off the Cotentin Peninsula before seizing the port of Cherbourg, and also connect the US forces with the British forces attacking on adjacent Gold Beach to the north-east. Omaha and Gold beaches would occupy the centre of the Normandy enclave and both were scheduled to receive the prefabricated Mulberry offshore docking harbours. Omaha was also to provide immediate access into the interior of the French countryside. Its realisation was essential, but its difficulty would verify the fears of all who dreaded and worried over the success of the entire invasion.

Although the Allied high command knew in advance that Omaha would be the most difficult of the five beaches, reconnaissance briefings and preparations had overcome their doubts and fears with three assumptions: 1.) the beach would only be defended by a makeshift and undermanned regiment of low calibre, poorly trained defenders; 2.) the invaders would possess overwhelming numbers of soldiers who would be accompanied by fully amphibious armoured tanks and quickly supported by motorised armoured weapons to provide immediate beach firepower to disable any German resistance; and 3.) the air and naval bombardment would have reduced the defending strong points to rubble. Any leftover defences would be quickly overwhelmed by the huge strength in numbers possessed by the invasion teams and their equipment. Unfortunately, all three assumptions would be proven incorrect.

The Germans had reinforced Omaha with a veteran division of well-trained soldiers, meaning more and better prepared defenders. The numbers of Allied soldiers reaching the beach proved to be slower in arriving and encountered greater difficulty reaching their designated sites due to the weather and wave conditions. Troops arriving were further reduced when many landing craft swamped or missed their landing points altogether, leading to confusion and a smaller trickle of reinforcing units. The ride to the beach was a traumatic and dangerous experience in itself due to the wave and sea conditions. Soldiers were frequently dazed, confused, seasick and under immediate and intense gunfire. It was a wicked combination of conditions. Very few of the amphibious armoured vehicles made it to the shore due to the strength of the waves and the fragility of the flotation devices, many of them becoming swamped, their crews drowning. Finally, the air and naval bombardment failed to be heavy enough or accurate enough and the German positions were mainly intact and fully operational. Such were the opening conditions confronting the first soldiers who hit the beach at Omaha.

On Omaha Beach it was the fighting soldiers who, after their perilous and nausea-inducing journey across the English Channel, now had to board their bobbing landing craft and set out into the storm-tossed low tide water at 06:30 on 6 June 1944 and begin their assault. The first wave at Omaha was assigned an initial strength of fifty LCVP (landing craft vehicles and personnel) with about one quarter of them British craft with British crews. Each boat carried at least thirty-one soldiers, for an arrival landing force of about 1,550 GIs landing on 4½ miles of beach. They exited their landing craft and entered a cauldron of rolling waves in water deeper than expected and a torrent of German gunfire – accurate and immediate. Typical was the report of this Coast Guard Higgins landing boat crewman, Electrician's Mate Alfred Sears, as his craft landed on Omaha Beach: 'We hit the sandbar, dropped the ramp, and then all hell poured loose on us. The soldiers in the boat received a hail of machine-gun bullets. [The] army lieutenant was immediately killed, shot through the head.'[17]

Private Charles Neighbor of the 29th Division succinctly described his observation on arrival at Omaha: 'As our boat touched sand and the ramp went down I became a visitor to hell.'[18] Fittingly, this view and observation elicited an identical quote from Private Harry Parley of the 16th Regiment, 1st Division.[19]

Those that reached shore alive were, not surprisingly, dazed and confused. The reality faced by those who managed to hit the beach intact and unhurt was chaos and uncertainty over where to go, what to do, and how to avoid enemy gunfire that was everywhere. Sergeant Thomas Valance reached the beach and clambered out of his Higgins boat only to wonder what was going on:

As we came down the ramp, we were in water about knee-high and started to do what we were trained to do, that is, move forward and then crouch and fire. One problem was we didn't quite know what to fire at. I saw some tracers coming from a concrete emplacement which, to me, looked mammoth. I never anticipated a gun emplacement being that big. I shot at it but there was no way I was going to knock out a German concrete emplacement with a .30 caliber rifle.[20]

According to PFC John Robertson, Company F, 116th Infantry, 29th Division:

I went in carrying 60 lbs. of ammunition of 60mm mortar ammo. My mortar crew was [wiped] out. There was a tank coming up behind me as I was lying in the water and across the beach and that got me up…it looked like suicide [but] I ran forward, and it was crazy, but better than getting run over.[21]

Pvt. George Kobe of Company D, 116th Infantry, 29th Division recalled:

I was with my mortar platoon in the landing craft with Capt. Walter Schilling. Suddenly I heard a German 88' whiz through the craft, ripping off the ramp and blowing off both steel doors of the LCA. The right door hit Capt. Schilling in the head, killing him instantly. The left door hit our platoon sergeant, John Stinnett, and he was blinded in one eye. Only an 88' could be that mean. There was no panic. How we made it through to the seawall, I'll never know. It was the worst fire I was ever subjected to in all of my time in combat.[22]

Up and down the beach, the story of arriving landing craft was the same: the ramp coming down and the Germans firing directly into the opened can of unshielded unloading soldiers, sometimes killing the entire contingent with one spray of heavy machine-gun fire. Sergeant Harry Bare's boat met a similar circumstance when his lead officer, who was positioned at the front of the boat by the ramp, was killed instantly as the ramp was lowered. Bare remembers:

As the ranking non-com, I tried to get my men off the boat and make it somehow to get under the seawall. We waded to the sand and threw ourselves down and the men were frozen, unable to move. My radioman had his head blown off three yards from me. The beach was covered with bodies, men with no legs, no arms – God it was awful.[23]

Bare and only six others of his boatload managed to reach the seawall alive. 'I was soaking wet, shivering, but trying like hell to keep control. I could feel the cold fingers of fear grip me.'[24] Typical too was the arrival of a Higgins boat led by Captain Ettore Zappacosta, who as leader was first down the ramp and instantly hit in the hip and shoulder. A medic immediately tended to him, only to be shot dead also. Every man on the landing craft was soon shot dead or wounded except Private Robert Sales.[25]

For those who survived the violent arrival, the water could provide an equally dangerous fate. Jumping over the side of a sinking Higgins boat and plunging into the shallow water while burdened with 60–100 pounds of equipment meant being pulled under the surf and drowning. Reaching the beach with their encumbering equipment hampered men's ability to go forward and seek cover from the withering German gunfire. Men dumped their equipment on the beach in order to scramble to safety behind steel and timber obstacles and then made a reckless run to the seawall for shelter and a chance to organise with anyone left alive. This abandoned equipment later became beneficial as further landing groups arrived at higher tide, dumped their gear in order to avoid drowning, waded or swam to shore then retrieved abandoned weapons and gear as they too advanced across the beach to the seawall and beyond.

The 29th Regimental Combat Team (RCT) of the 1st Division arrived at the wrong beach area with little or no support from accompanying armour and engineers: the former to provide firepower and armoured protection, the latter to clear obstacles and mines to allow the armour and infantry units to cross the beach. Unfortunately, the arrival of amphibious armour was an immediate disaster. Released beyond the designated drop point and in very deep and rough water, of the thirty-four amphibious tanks assigned to the initial run onto Omaha Beach, twenty-nine sank or failed and, tragically, drowned most of their crew with them.

The limited successes of DD (Duplex-Drive) tanks reaching the beaches intact came in the first delivery group, the two companies of the 743rd Tank Battalion. It was jointly agreed that the sea was too rough for the landing craft to unload the tanks in the deep surf, so instead the LCTs attempted to deliver the DDs onto the beach proper. Of this group, forty of forty-four tanks with the wading tank modification landed on the shore, although the ferocious defensive fire of the German guns immediately knocked out many of those that had landed and attempted to move forward. In the 741st Tank Battalion, the decision was made to launch 5,000 yards out to sea and the result for these two companies was the loss of twenty-seven of thirty-two tanks in one company and thirty of forty-eight tanks in another. In all, the amphibious armour delivery and support on Omaha Beach was virtually a total failure, in planning, operation and result – both in terms of the mission of seizing the beach and of the tragic loss of life to the armoured crews and to the infantry they were unable to support.

The run from the transports to the beach was over 25,000 yards (roughly 15 miles) of storm-tossed sea, leaving at least half of the attacking soldiers, who had already suffered a day's wait in the stormy English Channel, seasick and hardly fit for what they had to endure on the beach. Many were willing to brave the German gunfire just to get out of the wretched Higgins boats and their overwhelming and seemingly endless condition of seasickness, as expressed by Sergeant Benjamin McKinney, combat engineer in C Company, 116th Division, who like many others anxiously departed the Higgins craft. When his ramp dropped, 'I was so seasick I didn't care if a bullet hit me between the eyes and got me out of my misery … rifle and machine-gun fire hit it like rain falling … it looked as if all the first wave were dead on the beach.'[26]

The low tide landing left the attacking soldiers 300 yards of gun-raked and mine-infested beach to negotiate, before having to move up another 100 yards across enfilading crossfire to the semi-shelter of the beach bluff/shelf, but directly underneath the German concrete encased gun-posts and bunkers. If they survived, the GIs now faced a tangle of barbed wire, booby traps and landmines, and all in the face of the German 88s and machine guns. It was not a happy picture. The few survivors who managed to find some shelter under the bluff were totally stymied in attempting to return any gunfire, especially lacking any armour support.

It was at this point that numerous offshore destroyer commanders, already dangerously close to shallows and shore, decided to bring their shallower draft vessels in ever tighter to the beach to begin pounding the German positions with a hurricane of 5-inch gunfire. Once again, it was clear that the initial heavy naval bombardment had been inadequate in both number of big gun ships, and in the amount and accuracy of their targeting. In addition, low clouds had also prevented the air bombardment prior to the landings from accurately identifying and completely destroying the German gun positions. Air bombardment units had worried over how to accurately target beach positions, fearing friendly fire damage. Lifting their bomb target area, they released their bombs deeper behind the German lines in order to interdict any reinforcements, but consequently allowing beach defences to remain virtually intact.

The combination of inadequate naval and air bombardment, the loss of nearly all the amphibious armour before even arriving on the beach, the unexpected quality and size of the German defensive strength in terms of guns and defenders and the difficulty of the flat terrain of the Omaha Beach shelf in front of the high bluffs that provided little or no protection – all these became the perfect combination of conditions for disaster. Many died in the rising tide before ever hitting the beach, drowning or being shot while attempting to navigate the surf and locate footing for life-supporting ground beneath their feet, constantly confronted by a fiendish blizzard of machine-gun bullets from three sides. It was indeed hell.

With more waves of reinforcing attackers hitting the beach and being killed or wounded, the tangle of confusion, chaos and frustration amid the teeming death and destruction of the German gunfire demanded some sort of organisation. Obviously the initial plans and placement of soldiers and equipment was now completely derelict. As the Supreme Commander, General Eisenhower, had remarked repeatedly, 'Plans are everything before the battle, but useless once the battle is joined.' He and his staff had done all that they could possibly do leading up to D-Day, but now that the battle had begun, it would take on its own identity and rely on the skill, courage and determination of the soldiers and sailors involved. Training, planning and preparation could do only so much; the day would now be determined by real people, in desperate situations, with life and death on the line.

The troops who had survived were often leaderless, terrified and without any direction. Those in command, or those assuming leadership roles, no matter what their rank, realised that remaining on the beach was certain death and that moving forward to a more defendable position while forwarding the attack was the most prudent thing to do. It can be summarised by the words of Colonel Charles Canham, commanding the 116th Regiment of the 1st Infantry Division, when he urged those around him to move forward because, 'They're murdering us here [so] let's move inland and get murdered!'[27] Such was the sense of overwhelming futility for those who had survived the terrifying initial ordeal of the landing. Recognising their dire situation, the first task had been survival, followed by confusion over where to go and what to do given their precarious position on the beach. Gradually, and with grim determination, many began to reorganise what men and equipment were available and then somehow begin the elimination of the German gun positions that were pinning them down and preventing oncoming reinforcements from moving up.

For forty-seven-year-old Colonel George A. Taylor, commander of the 16th Infantry Regiment, the answer was obvious. On the beach, enduring mortar and shell fire and suffering casualties, Taylor arrived and starkly summed up the situation to those hugging the embankment for dear life: 'Two kinds of people are staying on this beach, the dead, and those who are going to die – now let's get the hell out of here'.[28]

For a time, however, so tenuous and desperate was the situation that General Omar Bradley, in overall command of the Omaha and Utah Beach sectors, seriously considered pulling the attacking units off of Omaha and withdrawing from that section of the invasion. Plans, objectives, positions – all were out the window. But the desperation would be overcome group by group, as each individual cluster of surviving soldiers formed with others to attack and destroy a machine-gun nest or bunker in their vicinity. Through the independent courage and heroism of individuals, a few would begin to lead while others gained enough confidence to follow and gradually the weight of more men, supported by more armoured units continuing to arrive, began to provide a toehold that evolved into a foothold.

Such an example of sheer courage and determination was exemplified by the assistant commander of the 29th Division, Brigadier General Norman Cota. Cota's aide-de-camp Lieutenant J. T. Shea vividly describes how the American quality of salvaging an answer to a seemingly hopeless situation took shape. Shea wrote:

Although the leading elements of the assault had been on the beach for approximately an hour, none had progressed farther than the seawall at the inland border of the beach. [They] were clustered under the wall, pinned down by machine gun fire, and the enemy was beginning to bring effective mortar fire to bear on those hidden behind the wall … [Cota] … exposing himself to enemy fire … went over the seawall giving encouragement, directions, and orders to those about him, personally supervised the placing of a BAR [Browning Automatic Rifle] and brought fire to bear on some of the enemy positions on the bluff that faced them. Finding a belt of barbed wire inside the seawall, General Cota personally supervised placing a Bangalore torpedo for blowing the wire and was one of the first three men to go through the wire.[29]

With increased and effective naval gunfire from offshore warships, the foothold of a few grew into a stronghold of many that began the reduction and elimination of German resistance.

This was how it was done, repeated up and down the smoky and death-strewn beach full of wrecked equipment: small groups of GIs, led by the courageous actions of gallant individuals of all ranks, took charge and somehow succeeded in doing what plans and diagrams on maps did not foresee or imagine. It had been costly, but Omaha Beach was secured by afternoon and under American control. It had not been easy or painless, but it had been accomplished.

American landing craft and soldiers on Omaha Beach wading through the surf and among the obstacles, with obvious heavy gun fire. (US Coast Guard)

American soldiers being pulled from the surf on Omaha Beach. (US Army)

Wounded Americans taking cover beneath sheltering cliffs. (US Army)

Sherman wading tanks moving ashore through the obstacles at Omaha Beach under heavy gunfire. Lack of immediate armour support contributed to the heavy casualties and near failure at Omaha Beach. (US Coast Guard)

This is the broad, tranquil shoreline from the high bluffs overlooking Omaha Beach today. (RJP)

Wounded and dead soldiers being tended at Omaha Beach. On D-Day the Allies suffered over 10,000 combined casualties on the five invasion beaches, with over 4,400 killed. The German casualty estimates range between 5,000 and 9,000. (US Army)

American M-10 tank destroyers coming ashore on the freshly captured Omaha Beach. The need to rapidly reinforce the captured position with soldiers and equipment was an essential component of the invasion plan. It was a race between the Allies and the defending Germans as to who could reinforce faster. (US Navy)

GIs of the US 2nd Infantry Division climbing the bluffs of the newly captured Omaha Beach. (US Army)

An early wave of assaulting infantry, under intense gunfire, at the outset of the Omaha Beach invasion. (NARA)

An aerial view of the Omaha Beach landings shortly after the beach was secured. (NARA)

Numerous LSTs unloading heavy equipment onto the recently acquired Normandy beaches, providing massive amounts of equipment and supplies as the Allied army prepared to march inland. (US Coast Guard)

A fully loaded Higgins boat, damaged and giving off smoke, continues on to the shore of Omaha Beach. (US Coast Guard)

The captured beach late in the afternoon of D-Day. A dead GI is seen on Omaha Beach, one of around 2,000 Americans killed taking Utah and Omaha beaches, the majority (probably around 1,500) on Omaha. Utah Beach suffered less than 200 killed; however, another roughly 350 airborne troops were killed fighting behind the beach. (NARA)

Chapter 12

Conclusion

Not to conquer any territory, not for any ambitions of our own. But to make sure that Hitler could not destroy freedom in the world.

> General Dwight Eisenhower reflecting back on what D-Day represented.

The English Channel had stranded Napoleon Bonaparte's Grande Army on the continental mainland in 1803–05, and that same moat of water had protected England against an invasion by Hitler and the Germans in 1940. However, in the spring of 1944, it failed to prevent Hitler's occupied Europe from being successfully invaded by the combined Allied forces. The Allies had prepared long, carefully and methodically; they had built up overwhelming resources to be projected by a mighty 7,000-ship fleet carrying over 150,000 soldiers while shielded with an invincible air umbrella of over 7,500 airplanes. But the greatest Allied asset was will: the will to expend the effort, energy, cost and pain of sacrifice on a crusade that was not only militarily necessary but truly morally correct and righteous – the elimination of Adolf Hitler and his Nazi regime's stranglehold over Europe. The Allied cause confronted seemingly insurmountable obstacles that were overcome at all stages of the Overlord operation: from agreement and approval, to planning, to staging. Finally came the most demanding challenge of all, the actual determined effort to seize five strongly defended beaches protected by the German Wehrmacht, which was equally determined to hold at any cost Hitler's Fortress Europe.

From their 50-mile-wide beachhead, the Allies funnelled prodigious quantities of resources, equipment and reinforcements into a race to see if they or the Germans could more quickly and heavily fortify their position. In fact, the logjam on the beaches with arriving men and equipment soon became a traffic hindrance as the growing support effort remained awkard to manage until more forward territory could be seized and the initial position broadened. This would take two weeks of hard fighting on the western edge up the Cotentin Peninsula, and over six weeks to gain the important French junction town of Caen on the British eastern flank. Enlarging a wider front ever further forward would allow ever greater numbers of troops and support to further expand the perimeter, while setting the stage for a breakout into the heart of France.

Planting their foot into Normandy was only a prelude, as the Germans still possessed a potent and powerful army – an army that was rightly respected by the Allies. For four years the Germans had prepared their Atlantic Wall with mines, obstacles and big gun beach defences and, although that had now been pierced, Hitler's Fortress Europe still retained roughly fifty-eight divisions, including ten Panzer armoured divisions. Stationed in reserve in order to hurl back an invasion or challenge the coastal landing, these forces were now poised to pounce upon the narrow enclave holding the Allied position. Even as the Allies immediately sought to reinforce following their successful landing, they were initially only able to wedge six divisions, plus three airborne divisions, onto the narrow Normandy beachhead. Reinforcement would double the numbers of troops and resources within a week, but the Allies still faced daunting challenges in having to repeatedly cross the stormy English Channel, land more divisions of men and armour and rapidly expand their positions before moving across France to drive the Nazis back into Germany. This they eventually succeeded in doing. Again, it demanded preparation, determination and implementation – it was a masterful performance on all levels but not without a hint of failure, as witnessed by the near debacle on Omaha Beach in the early phases of the assault.

Next would be the grinding advance of General Bernard Montgomery and the British on the key town of Caen; the envelopment of the Cotentin Peninsula by the Americans from Utah Beach; and the arduous American progress from Omaha Beach through the tangled rows of hedges lining the French farmland known as Bocage. These centuries-old bushes and hedges made a perfect hiding place for the dangerous German Panzer units as they repeatedly ambushed and thwarted American efforts to penetrate and advance. Only through the determined and creative tactics of the American armoured units were the Americans able to root out the hidden German defenders. By cleverly adapting large steel-pronged forks onto the nose of their tanks to pierce the bushy hedges, the Americans were able to penetrate the Bocage barriers and drive forward from Omaha Beach. Following a massive build-up of strength, the next phase would be the near total envelopment of the defending German Army. Eventually, the American units on the western flank north of Utah Beach would break through the German defences, swing north and east and surround the Germans in an area that would come to be known as the Falaise Pocket. It would be a stunning Allied victory, opening the door to crossing northern France and liberating Paris.

This breakout occurred almost precisely as German Field Marshal Erwin Rommel had predicted: once established, the Allies were able to connect their beaches, deepen their holding position, reinforce their assault troops and expand their lodging. There was at that point little the Germans could do except to repeatedly counterattack, which they urgently did. But Montgomery's eastern left wing held and drove on to capture the town of Caen, chewing up German reinforcements in the process. From the west, the Americans under General George Patton's Third Army swung around the pivot and sprang a noose around the German positions, surrounding their entire army and nearly bagging the whole lot. As it was, a greater part of the German units and equipment was annihilated in the Falaise Pocket. Some German elements were able to escape, but the breach opened the plains of France to a rapid advance and the liberation of Paris. Pulling back in retreat, the Germans were forced to re-establish their position in a more defensible location that the Allies would struggle to break through during the remainder of 1944. But the die was cast. It was only a matter of time (and lives) before the overwhelming resources of the Allies would surmount the desperate Germans, driving them back across the Rhine and into the heartland of Germany proper, where in May 1945 the American and British forces would link up with the Soviets and force the surrender of Hitler's now devastated 'Thousand Year Reich'.

Without a doubt, had the D-Day incursion been thrown back into the sea, the course of the war would have been seriously altered. Perhaps the Soviet Red Army would have driven through Germany and into France, occupying even more of post-Second World War Europe before the Allies could recover and attempt to reinvade. Churchill had predicted that, 'once Stalin's forces [the Red Army] were in a country, it would be impossible to remove them', and that proved to be true for the next forty-five years of the Cold War.[30] Had the invasion been postponed another two weeks, it would have coincided with 'the Great Storm' of 19–22 June. Lasting three days, the worst Channel storm in forty years would have certainly destroyed the invasion attempt and perhaps prevented it from taking place even later that summer.

But Overlord did succeed, in spite of its setbacks and difficulties in execution, and in the face of all the various 'what-ifs' that could have emerged to wreck the invasion. Still to come would be the demanding drive through France at a cost of 125,000 American casualties. Another 85,000 Allied casualties would result while decimating the remaining German defences, with over 250,000 German casualties and another 200,000 Germans captured. And all this loss of life would take place before the brutal Battle of the Bulge and the ensuing final conquering march into Germany. It was a bitter and violent end, but the Western Allies of Britain and the US would cross the Rhine and occupy one-half of Germany, setting the stage for the next generation of conflict and crisis. Before the Second World War had even been concluded came rumblings of a Cold War with our former allies, the Soviet Russians, who now occupied half of Europe. One tyrannical totalitarian regime was being replaced by another, but at least France and Western Europe had been liberated from tyranny. For that, we can thank D-Day.

It had been a struggle and a costly one, and looking back from the twenty-first century, the result may now seem more inevitable than it truly was. But the testimony of the participants reveals the vivid concern and ominous threat of failure. Their words and deeds speak to us through the decades, reminding us of the impending trial that lay before those who fought and endured this effort. It required the resolve, the courage, the stamina, and the sheer determination to believe in their cause and to stand up to the challenge – to embark on Operation Overlord and the Allied invasion of Western Europe on D-Day, 6 June 1944.

German soldiers surrendering to American tanks in the French Bocage area. (NARA)

The wrecked Mulberry port at Omaha Beach after the 'Great Storm' of 19–21 June. This Mulberry was never repaired. (US Navy)

Wrecked and destroyed German units in the Falaise Pocket. (US Army)

American soldiers fighting in the difficult French Bocage region. ((NARA)

An American M-10 tank destroyer firing on a German position. (US Army)

Above: Destroyed German tanks along a French road in the Falaise Pocket. (NARA)

Right: General George Patton, commander of the American 3rd Army. Patton's units swept around the American right (western) flank to encircle the German defenders, trapping and destroying virtually the entire German force within the Falaise Pocket. (US Army)

Americans on parade in the newly liberated city of Paris. It was the Normandy invasion, Operation Overlord, that made this achievement possible. (LOC)

The American Military Cemetery at Colleville-sur-Mer, overlooking Omaha Beach. The cemetery contains the graves of over 9,000 American soldiers killed during the campaign in France. (RJP)

Bibliography

Ambrose, Stephen E., *D-Day: The Climactic Battle*, Simon & Schuster (1994).

Badsey, Stephen, *Normandy 1944*, Osprey Publishing (1990).

Balkowski, Joseph, *Omaha Beach, D-Day June 6, 1944*, Stackpole Books (2004).

Beevor, Anthony, *D-Day: The Battle for Normandy*, Viking Penguin Books (2009).

Berthon, Simon and Joanna Potts, *Warlords*, Da Capo Press (2006).

Brinkley, Douglas and Ronald Drez, *Voices of Valor*, Bullfinch Press (2004).

Budiansky, Stephen, *Air Power*, Penguin Books (2004).

Ford, Ken and Steven Zaloga, *Overlord: The D-Day Landings*, Osprey Publishing (2009).

Gelb, Norman, *Ike and Monty*, William Morrow (1994).

Hanson, Victor Davis, *The Second World Wars*, Basic Books (2017).

Hall, Anthony, *D-Day, Day by Day*, Chartwell Books (2012).

Jordan, Jonathan, *American Warlords*, Penguin Books (2015).

Keegan, John, *Six Armies in Normandy*, Penguin Books (1982).

Messenger, Charles, *The D-Day Atlas*, Thames & Hudson (2004).

Overy, Richard, *The Bombers and the Bombed*, Penguin Books (2013)

Penrose, Jane (ed.), *The D-Day Companion*, Osprey Publishing (2004).

Perry, Mark, *Partners in Command*, Penguin Books (2007).

Symonds, Craig L., *Neptune*, Oxford University Press (2014).

Tillman, Barrett, *D-Day Encyclopedia*, Regnery History (2014).

Van der Vat, Dan, *D-Day: The Greatest Invasion*, Bloomsbury (2003).

Endnotes

1. Keegan, *Six Armies*, p. 55
2. Ibid, pp. 296–297 or Beevor, *D-Day*, pp. 16–21 and 200
3. Badsey, Stephen, *Normandy, 1944*, pp. 15–16
4. Ambrose, *D-Day*, p. 113
5. Tillman, *D-Day Encyclopedia*, p. 267
6. Ford and Zalaga, *Overlord: The D-Day Invasions*, pp. 54–56
7. Budiansky, *Air Power*, p. 303
8. Keegan, *Six Armies*, p. 59
9. Ambrose, *D-Day*, p. 251
10. Ibid, p. 251
11. Overy, *The Bombers and the Bombed*, p. 387
12. Ibid, pp. 390–391
13. Ibid, p. 391
14. Ibid, p. 392
15. Budiansky, *Air Power*, p. 300
16. Ibid, pp. 302–303
17. Ambrose, *D-Day*, p. 326
18. Murray, *D-Day Companion*, p. 118
19. Ambrose, *D-Day*, p. 335
20. Ibid, p. 328
21. Balkowski, *Omaha Beach*, p. 126
22. Ibid, p. 160
23. Ambrose, *D-Day*, p. 331
24. Ibid, p. 332
25. Ibid, p. 337
26. Ibid, p. 338
27. Tillman, *D-Day Encyclopedia*, p. 265
28. 'War Dept. Historical Division – Omaha Beach' pp. 43–59
29. Ambrose, *D-Day*, p. 339
30. Berthon and Potts, *Warlords*, p. 266

Index